Hip &

Hidden

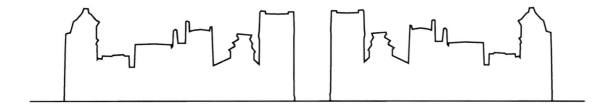

Hip & Hidden Philadelphia
The unexpected house in a city of tradition

Virginia Restemeyer & E. I. Weiner

Probasco Haus Press

Dedicated to the Hip & Hidden Philadelphians among us, those who have set the bar for dreaming and doing. They are followers of their own personal visions and interpretations of "home place," whether as experimenters, hired professionals or expressive residents, and despite the difficulties encountered when stepping outside the Philadelphia box.

And to our Four Feline Guys, the antithesis of elves, who slept next to us while we did all the work. They were great unconscious companions whose heaving purrs made it all worthwhile. We wish they were here to see the finished book. They would express indifference to it but flatter us anyway.

Probasco Haus Press
P.O. Box 41045
Philadelphia, Pennsylvania 19127
www.probascohauspress.com

ISBN: 978-0-9766626-2-4

Typeset in Gill Sans
Printed in the United States of America by The HF Group

Acknowledgments: Thanks to Jonathan E. Farnham, Executive Director of the City of Philadelphia Historical Commission (who was a staff member when we started this project); Donna Carter, a hugely helpful and patient records librarian at the Philadelphia Department of Licenses and Inspections; Laura Jacoby and Susan DiGironimo, both excellent graphic designers who taught Photoshop and Quark classes at Rosemont College, and who we hope would approve of our attempts; Apple Computers, for many things, but for creating an operating system that is not only graphically friendly, but which makes all things possible; both sets of parents – Hilda and Sam, and Virginia and William – for making us open and curious; and Miriam Mednick, for being an early adopter and creator of a revitalized Center City carriage house, and who set a lovely tone for others to follow.

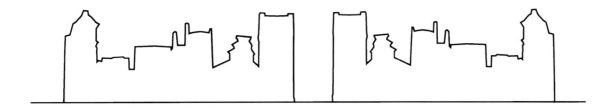

CONTENTS

Introduction	*4*
The Classics	*11*
Adaptive Reuse	*25*
The Incorporated Past	*39*
Facelift	*55*
Pioneers	*69*
Quirky Individualism	*81*
House = Site	*93*
Artistic Assertion	*105*
Modernist Assertion	*121*
The Referenced Past	*139*
Unique, No Comparables	*151*
Neighborhood Guide	*168*
Architects Guide	*169*
Selected Bibliography	*173*

INTRODUCTION

Yes, Philadelphia is old, and historic, and in many ways still defined by its Quaker reticence and aversion to appearing showy. Those are all true descriptors, to one degree or another; inarguably, some of those traits are what make the city interesting, even endearing. Certainly, they are chief among the characteristics that make the city promotable, especially to the tourist trade. After all, the advertising mascot for the city's tourism office has been an actor dressed up to look like Benjamin Franklin; tour guides are costumed in Colonial-era garb. It is not the geographical center, but Independence Hall is certainly the identity center, and one from which few visitors wander far. Outsiders see the city as another Williamsburg, a planned and controlled place designed to help us appreciate how our forebears lived and how our nation was shaped; the local chapter of the American Institute of Architects itself calls the city "an expansive outdoor museum." Even natives would, if pressed, probably describe Philadelphia in historic terms and Revolutionary War time frames. The overall message given and impression received is that what is worth looking at here is brick and cobblestone and at least 250 years old.

Unquestionably, lately, Philadelphia has shown itself to be a burgeoning contemporary city as well. It has a lively nightlife, world-class restaurants, new stadiums, a vibrant youth culture, a casually accepted diversity and a viable downtown that is the envy of most big American cities. A boom of tall, glittery and stylish condominium buildings has been popping up all over town, adding to a heightened level of enthusiasm and self-congratulation; some critics have remarked that these modern structures herald a new Philadelphia, one ready to burst free from the chains of the old and embrace the modern as the new civic ethos.

These definitions and borderlines – that of the limiting old and the suddenly freewheeling new, with nothing in-between – sell Philadelphia and its cityscape, and the history of both, short. There is more to the story.

Inside Philadelphia there is another Philadelphia, and it has been there for quite some time. This other Philadelphia is subtle and subversive; it has been the true sign of a different way of thinking. It has nothing to do with condominium or apartment buildings, or commercial skyscrapers – the sorts of construction that garner the greatest news coverage and critical analysis. It has, rather, everything to do with the essential building block of Philadelphia, the thing that makes it a city of neighborhoods and neighbors: the house.

As we, the authors, walked through our city we were struck by the random and sudden, utterly unexpected and fully rewarding sight of houses that are not the norm, not in keeping with the overwhelming thematic style of 18th- and 19th-century houses that is much of Philadelphia, and yet not the anonymous, boilerplate, bland structures, unadorned and unlovable, that went up primarily in the second half of the 20th century – not the "city of housing developments" that writer Thomas Hine says Philadelphia is, since "nearly all of the city's housing was built in multiple units by commercial developers."

What we are speaking of are the different ones, the unique ones, the one-of-a-kind ones. There are a few here, one or two there, but, if not in profusion, they are to be found in nearly every part of town. We have always been drawn to these unique offerings because they were divergent and "outsider," and successful in connecting with those characteristics, awake or dormant, within the viewer; also, because they exhibited a kind of playful iconoclasm in contrast to their context. These are not, we hurry to add, the newer minidevelopments erected by excited young designer/builders experimentally using European styles of aesthetics or efficiency in large or small housing clusters in rapidly rehabbing neighborhoods. What we have been drawn to, rather, are those houses – single houses, or, at most, two or three together – that went up in places and at times when doing so wasn't as easy or welcome or likely as it is today.

Our feeling is that cultures and nations are not shaped by the many but, rather, by the few: those with a vision and the drive to work toward it and express it despite the consequences. The founding of America, after all, is about rebellion, not conformity. In our city, so steeped in an architectural tradition, there are pockets of rebellion, glimpses of individual expression that serve as guideposts to the future. Don't misunderstand – we treasure the historic buildings in this city that provide a character and charm that is irreplaceable and unique, without which we would not have the "others." We love both – the well-known, overriding zeitgeist of the colonial new world and its succeeding style generations up to and through the 19th century, as well as the sporadic inexplicable anomalies that make our city that much richer and unduplicatable.

As we walked, we started seeing more of these different places. We wondered if there might not be some thread or connection – some visual, thematic or theoretical similarities that strung these residential gems together. We wondered if this might represent a phenomenon or, instead, indicate a movement: a domino effect of either purposeful or subconscious influence, or a completely unrelated array of coincidences – or, perhaps, something about the personality of the city that made these houses possible, even necessary.

We decided to explore the possibilities. What we found, after years of looking, is what we have come to call "hip and hidden Philadelphia."

WHAT IS HIP? WHAT IS HIDDEN?

Why call these houses "hip" and "hidden," and what, exactly, do these terms mean when applied to Philadelphia residences?

"Hidden" is the easier concept to explain. With a few of the houses, this is a nearly literal description: One lies at the end of a long drive where it is then camouflaged behind tall bushes, another seems to duck behind a forbidding stockade fence, while yet another sits incongruously atop an ignorable multistory warehouse building. These, and others, are truly, in the active sense, hiding from the view of passersby.

Considered hidden, too, are houses in the alleyways, tiny streets, one-block alcoves and service driveways that very few people, even natives and neighbors, wander down. To extend that definition, "hidden" describes locations that are "off the beaten path": not along the busier commercial boulevards, away from the tourist trails, out of the main business corridors. In other words, you have to make an effort to find them, and if you don't know they're there, you would have no reason to go look.

Since the houses of interest in this book are few and far between, they are hidden by sheer lack of numbers, needles in the gigantic haystack that is the city, including those places found by the authors not just in the core of the city but also on lush wooded lots that reclaim the architecture thrust upon them, in unlikely neighborhoods of neglect and poverty, in otherwise homoge-

neous and solidly working-class blocks where decorative ironwork has been the sign of a household's prosperity and on once-vacant lots redeveloped by the housing authority.

Oddly, and almost magically, a number of the selections are what can only be described as being hidden in plain sight; that is, they stand on fairly well traveled streets, are large, are substantially unlike anything in their immediate context … and, yet, they are generally ignored, unnoticed, as if they were not there at all, when in fact they are, if anything, very there. It is almost as if, by being so different, they create a gap of expectation, punching a hole in our perception of what that block ought to look like – almost as if our minds can't process the difference and so negate it. This strange disappearing act is made even more effective when the material and size of the hip and hidden house are similar to those of its immediate neighbors.

Finally, in the most macro terms, these houses may be considered hidden for the reason that Philadelphia, itself, is hidden as well. Because of its geographical fate to be located between the shinier destination spots of New York City and Washington, D.C., and because of its seemingly natural, though thoroughly unmerited, inferiority complex and self-denigration, Philadelphia is frequently referred to as a "best kept secret" or "underappreciated." Generally, then, the places in this book are among the best kept secrets within the best kept secret – quite hidden, indeed.

Defining "hip" is more difficult and elusive than pinning down "hidden," especially when it comes to architecture, and doubly especially when it comes to Philadelphia, which is, within and without, seldom considered hip in any way at all. (One is reminded of globe-trotting tennis great Martina Navratilova's depiction of cities in America: "In this big country, I can be as brash as New York, as hedonistic as Los Angeles, as sensuous as San Francisco, as brainy as Boston, as proper as Philadelphia, as brawny as Chicago, as warm as Palm Springs, as friendly as my adopted home town of Dallas, Fort Worth, and as peaceful as the inland waterway that rubs up against my former home in Virginia Beach." Other cities have strength or smarts or sensuousness; Philadelphia has rules, and follows them.)

One might turn to the dictionary to find the definiton of "hip," but it is entirely insufficient. "Familiar with the latest ideas, styles," it reads; "informed; knowledgeable … characterized by a particularly strong sense of alienation from most social intercourse and endeavor."

This isn't quite it at all. To come to some definition, or group of parameters, concerning the concept of "hip" to use in this book, certain questions were asked; they were not necessarily answered, but cut a path towards the goal. Some of the questions that guided and, ultimately, informed us were: Is there a universal "hip," or is it merely contextual? Is "hip" just another way of saying "maverick"? Is "hip" only a need to be different or to go against the norm, or is it a distinctive style of its own? Is it, perhaps, a style that owes much to previous thinking but uses the most current materials available to stake its own claim? Can there be a "hip style," or is that totally antithetical to the concept and thesis? (As Portland, Oregon-based architect Brad Cloepfil, of Allied Works, has stated, "If every banker tries to be hip, it kind of ruins hipness." Does that go for every architect, too?)

In looking at the houses in this book, and looking at the housing stock that they sit among, and, further, looking at the thousands of row and twin and single homes that make up Philadelphia – and contemplating the questions that the authors posed to themselves – here is what we think "hip" is, and how we used these definitions to shape this book..

"Hip" houses have a sense of what's been, what is and what's possible. "Hip" entails awareness of self, as well as an assertion of that self. It has design intelligence, modernity and, not infrequently, theatricality.

"Hipness" also has a playfulness that is often missing from "serious" architecture. It has an anti-preciousness, in addition to a willingness to take a risk, to take a stand. Its driving imperative, in the hands of those who build the "hip" houses, is to personalize impersonal space.

A "hip" house is one that is not "off the rack"; it is one that could be just as well the work of a great architect or of a passionate amateur, either one committed to taking a building out of the realm of the ordinary and making it a unique personal expression of the inhabitant or the designer. These houses are the visual result of idiosyncrasy: they have the "vision thing," and tread that fine line between "what were they thinking?" and "why didn't I think of that?"

Not every house in this book will display all these traits but most of them have many of them. What all those who have built these hip houses, or have reworked old houses in hip ways, have succeeded in doing, though, is adding another element, providing an additional item to the definition of "hip": bravery. To do, in Philadelphia, what they have in many cases done – to build an assertion of self, or of Modernism, or of iconoclasm, something totally out of line, out of style, opposed to the surrounding consensus, right in the middle of a row of 19th-century rowhouses – is to have taken a conservative tornado by the tail. To have succeeded in making that structure not only befit its surroundings, but in many cases outshine them – and making them fit in so well that they can actually be said to be hidden – goes beyond bravery into the realm of something akin to genius.

The "hip" part of the "hip and hidden" equation has much to do with positive attitude in the face of obstacles, and with the human propensity toward making one's environment one's own, of leaving a mark, even, perhaps, a legacy, without the need for it to be the tallest or costliest or any other

fame-game "-ests." This hipness is a bright spot, a gift to passersby and neighbors alike; in some ways, it is a selfless act, because what is good is not just inside, behind walls, available only for the inhabitants' personal pleasure. It is shared for all – lucky enough to find it – to see. Coming upon and taking the time to view and appreciate a "hip and hidden" house is like gazing into intelligent eyes and seeing that there is something there, a light of awareness, a flicker of promise, a hint of insouciance behind the baby blues.

ABOUT THE CRITERIA

Again, this is difficult to quantify. Most of the time it was simply a know-it-when-you-see-it experience, clear to both authors at once that a property fit the specifications perfectly – and not only fit them, but helped to define and refine them. At other times, there was debate. Sometimes a property was not hip enough, or hidden enough, or sometimes it was enough of one of those but not enough of the other. At other times, one author's "hip" was the other author's puzzlement over the first author thinking it was hip. There was no hard and fast checklist; there was no precise scientific scale. It was just knowing, at first; later, it was seeing places fall into developing categories and commonalities, which made the selection job easier and increasingly exciting. But this was no casual, superficial, "straight eye for the queer house," pop-culture ramble. The authors catalogued nearly two hundred properties and researched all of them, and finally, taking into account the physical and financial realities of the book, pared down the group to the essential buildings presented here. It is hoped that the worthy others that did not find their way into this volume will soon find a place in another. They are all remarkable.

The only hard and fast criterion was this: that the property had to lie within the Philadelphia city limits. There were numerous intriguing houses literally within short distance just outside the border, but it had been decided early in the process that the strict boundary of search and inclusion in this book was the city line. This was non-negotiable, although occasionally very tempting to renegotiate.

Beyond this, the buildings that made the cut had to be visible from the street although often obscured by context, by landscaping, by site position or by subtlety. They could be enhanced from the original or newly constructed. They needed to display a novel use of materials or color or form.

The authors were strongly committed to restricting inclusion in the book to houses, not larger buildings. For one, it is because the basis of Philadelphia architecture and city planning, the subatomic particle that gives the city its charge, is the single-family dwelling. Houses are the nouns and verbs of

Philadelphia's architectural language, for which we owe a grateful debt to Willian Penn. Moreover, houses tend to lend themselves to greater self-expression than a commercial project with a big budget and corporate clients (with both architects and clients possibly located out of city, and thus with little feel for it). Finally, houses can be designed, built and decorated by nonprofessionals, making them true grassroots means of self-expression.

Another reason we avoided including commercial properties in our search is that they are, by nature, antithetical to the "hip and hidden" concept: that is, it is in their best interests for doing business to avoid hiding themselves. In the pursuit of customers, the architects' attempts to make their buildings eye-catching are usually just superficial and cunning, without any real depth of expression or personality or, certainly, autobiography. How quickly, though, the hard and fast can become soft and unsettled when one falls in love with something, as the authors did for some businesses and storefronts that were just too pertinent, engaging and fun to leave out. A few of them appear in this volume, and are duly noted. It should be mentioned, though, that all of them have residential components to them, and are not fully commercial.

A final criterion was that beauty and cleverness alone were not sufficient; more central was that the buildings, in keeping with the overall hip and hidden concept, had either to be totally divergent from the perceived idea of "Philadelphia," or completely "Philadelphia" but in piecemeal, deconstructed or referential ways. In other words, Philadelphia was always the touchstone.

METHODOLOGY

We went out looking for buried treasure. We did, professionally, what we enjoy doing in everyday life – walking and noticing, finding and collecting – and formalized it. An early decision – kept throughout the project – was that we would travel to all sections of the city, walk the streets and view the properties as anyone walking those sidewalks would. The only difference was, we took photographs and copious descriptive notes. Again, to keep this book as one all about the impressions of discovery, we did not talk to the current residents of the homes, nor to those who lived in them before, except when confronted by the former when they saw us closely observing their homes for no apparent good reason, and then photographing them. In nearly every instance, we did not speak to the architects. Intention of the creator is one thing; what the creation says to the viewer is another. It is the latter that interested us, and led to this book. As musicians used to say, it's what's in the grooves that counts.

In the writing, furthermore, we decided to make the book one full of impressions, first and otherwise. In the text accompanying the photos, there are many comparisons and similes: houses are said to look like or feel like one thing or another; some of the properties were so rich and full of life or reference, or touched something within us, that they made us think of several things they were like, all at once, some of them odd or even contradictory. We put those impressions in because, when we thought them, they made us admire or love the buildings all the more for being like other things we admire or love, or are a part of our world. If a house can make a person think, even if in circumscribed ways of comparison, it is a house worthy of noting.

Because this book is about the appearance and context of residences, as can be seen by any walker in the city (with two exceptions, where we gained access to private grounds – something not available to every, or any, passerby – with the owners' permission), we excluded any attempt to see, any description of and most research about the buildings' interiors. That can be some other book some other time. This is a book for viewers, not voyeurs (although we admit to peeking through some front windows).

Once the selection process was completed, each building was researched using city records, including those from the Department of Licenses and Inspections and the Philadelphia Historical Commission. Contemporaneous and later news stories were referred to for details. Records of the Philadelphia Architects and Buildings Project – an information consortium composed of numerous city research institutions, libraries, museums, schools and historical societies, and found on the Internet at http://www.philadelphiabuildings.org – were an invaluable resource.

The authors applied for no grants, and received no funding. Nothing was promised, expected or preconditioned. This book was a labor of love, a personal journey of discovery and, as such, if read carefully, is as autobiographically redolent as a straight confession.

ABOUT THE PHOTOGRAPHS

The photographs in this book are not nor were they ever intended to be the sort of artfully awe-inspiring and impossibly perfect images one might see in a glitzy coffee-table book or a magazine like, say, National Geographic. We did not cart around crates of photographic equipment. We did not use lights, or even a tripod. We did not shoot from heights or at rare angles to get highly-composed and dramatic results. To the contrary: the photos in this book are snapshots, taken with a handheld digital camera, using available light (which on autumn and winter days and most afternoons wasn't very available). It was our intent to show the houses, warts and all, unaltered and unPhotoshop'ed, the way anyone would see them from the sidewalk, or across the street, or halfway down the block, with cars in front of them and utility wires strung across them. We felt we didn't have to shoot them in a fashion to make them appear to be works of art. They already are works of art, and just needed to be clearly, simply documented. We wanted to snap them and not draw too much attention to what we were doing. (It is remarkable how turning a lens on a usually unphotographed place draws owners and crowds, the former thinking the picture-taker is either a worker for a city licensing department or an insurance-claims adjuster, the latter wondering what was so intriguing or important about these places that they had never really noticed before.)

Also, to answer the question of why so many of these shots were taken in autumn and winter: Philadelphia is not only a city of houses, it is a city of houses with leafy curbside trees grown up right in front of them. It is one thing for a place to be hip and hidden; it is another thing to have a book full of photographs of trees and no discernible structures behind them. To see the houses, waiting for leaves to fall was a necessity. And, when reshoots were occasionally necessary, often a year needed to pass to get a second chance – sometimes, but not often, with a resulting change, over the course of that time, in paint colors and window decorations.

WHAT WE LEARNED

Facts, dates, our way around sections of the city we had never before visited, even knowledge of some building techniques – we learned all these along the way of this project. These were fine things to acquire, but certainly not of the highest importance.

We noted, too, that most of the examples of hip and hidden in the book are to be found either in the most economically viable sections of town or in neighborhoods in upward transition. No surprise, really.

We learned how to truly look and see – and the difference between the two – something we always thought we were not only good at but also professionally adept at. Working on this book honed our noticing and appreciating skills, which in turn led us to see the hip and hidden in houses we might not have. At first we were drawn to the most obvious and shockingly unique, but as we learned more through our explorations we found ourselves gravitating toward the small gesture, the subtleties. Though we started out personally favoring architecture from the early beginnings of the current age – that time-shift moment when designs became more fluid and streamlined and all was bathed in the golden glow of incandescent light – we learned to love even the cool, seemingly indifferent Modernist buildings because they, too, express feelings, if well done. Doing this book has opened our hearts as well as our eyes.

More importantly, in discovering the hip and hidden "other" Philadelphia, we learned that what makes a city a city, what makes a city a great city, and what makes a city not a suburb (with its conformity or, in its version of diversity, its several different forms of conformity; i.e., one builder's three models vs. another's three models of "custom" homes) is not just its multiplicity and diversity but its tolerance for them. Philadelphia might seem, and might want to seem, like a stick in the mud, but it is an ecosystem that can accept non-native invasives at the same time that it would appear, on surface, to want to yank them up by the roots for being inappropriately placed and fruitful.

The biggest lesson we learned in discovering and exploring hip and hidden Philadelphia is that a great city is not a place where people live – anywhere could be that – but it is rather a place where different kinds of people, with their different tastes, styles, goals and dreams, live in an embrace and celebration (or, at worst, a benign neglect) of their differentness. "We talk a great deal about placelessness in the United States, about the lack of a meaningful landscape," writes Nathaniel Popkin in *Song of the City*. "But the body of the city, to paraphrase Walt Whitman, contains our multitudes. It contains and reflects our individual desires."

WHAT WE HOPE THIS BOOK WILL DO

We hope that selecting and spotlighting these houses might bring a new perspective to them and other "outsiders" like them, and increase citizens' interaction with them and the appreciation of their value to the rich mix that is Philadelphia. We cannot let their newness and otherness get in the way. As writes Barbara Capitman about the historic Deco district of Miami, which she helped to champion and revive, in words that apply as well to hip and hidden Philadelphia: "Because this 'past' is so much more immediate than what most people consider 'history,' its reflection of ourselves is a more personal one. It makes us examine more closely the contexts of our lives, and see ourselves more clearly as the creators as well as the products of those contexts."

We hope that bringing attention to these houses will help to gain historic certification – and, therefore, a certain protection of their integrity – for many of these, or at least to create an atmosphere in which they would be taken seriously for such certification. In a city that honors its Colonials and Victorians, it is time to conserve and safeguard the irreplaceable gems of the 20th century, and now the 21st.

In aid of this, we would hope that focus on hip and hidden properties might lead to better noting, reporting and record-keeping about them and every significant residential structure in the city. Most of the houses in this book are less than a hundred years old, and yet one could conclude that they were constructed in misty prehistory for all the gaps and lack of documentation, either because they were never documented or that records have been ill-kept and misplaced. For houses built even within the past few decades there was spotty information in Licenses and Inspections files, little in Historical Commission archives, and skimpy, contradictory and downright incorrect information in news stories. This has to do with Philadelphia's architectural and social heritage; a better job of keeping the city's legacy must be done, and coordination among agencies must be encouraged.

One great hope is that this book will cause readers to reevaluate or discover, and, in either event, to give the proper honor to some of the great architects who have worked in and, in some cases, continue to work in Philadelphia. If this book does nothing else, we hope that it will give a greater general-public recognition to architects heretofore heralded only within their own professional circles: Harry Sternfeld (1888-1976), whose well-crafted and diverse work spans styles from Beaux Arts to Modern, and includes monumental works as well as daring residences; Frank Weise (1918-2003), a man of the arts who worked with both George Howe and Louis Kahn, and whose distinctive approach to structure and design led to many of the city's most singular and visionary architectural achievements; Adolf DeRoy Mark (1928-2008), whose modern take on period and regional styles, most prominently the vernacular of the American Southwest (where he relocated and practiced), provided Philadelphia with some of its most distinctive houses, chimneys and landmarks; Hans Egli (1925-2001), an unswerving champion of new design who was not intimidated by placing his striking Modernist structures in thoroughly traditional contexts; and Cecil Baker, who, alone and in various partnerships, has beautifully captured the essences and nuances of traditional Philadelphia architecture, then reimagined and refined them through a user-friendly Modernist filter. Others of the highest creative caliber also show up more than once in this book; to help in finding their work, we have included in the backmatter a list of architects keyed to the pages where their work appears.

Writer/editor John Leland points out in his book, *Hip: The History*, that the word "hip" comes from the language of African slaves: "hipt," in the Woloft tongue, means "to open one's eyes." And that is the point, the core and the hope of *Hip and Hidden Philadelphia*: to urge those who walk the city to open their eyes and see the marvels created by those who opened theirs, and who themselves were – and who, in turn, created something – hip; and to be, in the words of architect Otto Sperr, "an invitation to the pleasure of knowing what one is looking at – or of knowing what one has hurried past for many years … [the] ongoing galleries in which intense and personal communications are offered for the sensitive response of passersby."

WHAT THIS BOOK IS NOT (AND WHY THAT IS GOOD)

This book is not a tour book. On the other hand, it is not intended to be some moribund catalogue. It is designed to show you houses but not lead you to them, at least not directly. But it is meant to make you want to see them in the "flesh."

We have not included street addresses for two reasons. First, these houses are not exhibits in a museum, or theme-park rides, or even public buildings, though most sit along public byways. These are people's homes. The residents have much to be proud of, especially if they were in any way responsible for the construction or alteration of their places, and they are surely happy to receive compliments. But it is not their job to do so, and it may not be their pleasure to be spokespersons for their house, addressing questions and comments from those who, having seen the property in the book, have arrived at their door and knocked on it.

Second, and more importantly, we have not included the addresses of these houses because it is our hope that you will go explore on your own and find them, as we did, coming upon them, thrilled, surprised and even a bit emotional. At the end of the book we include a list of the houses and the general Philadelphia neighborhoods in which they can be found. We encourage the reader to go out looking. Take a walk. Wander the great neighborhoods of this great city. If you find these places, then we are happy for you. But if you walk all around, say, Chestnut Hill or Fitler Square and do not come across the houses in this book, we are certain that you will not have walked in vain; rather, you will certainly have come across other places that excite you, dazzle you, inform you or even give you ideas for your own house. We would like you to see the treasures we uncovered, but more, we would love for you to find your own, those houses that will become your secrets, to which you hold the treasure map – places that you will, with almost proprietary pride, show off to others. Put one foot in front of the other, take impulsive turns down unlikely streets and alleys, follow your instinct or give yourself up to chance, and you may find what we illustrate in these pages, or, very likely, and just as happily, your own hip and hidden Philadelphia.

Virginia Restemeyer
E. I. Weiner

A classic is classic not because it conforms to certain structural rules, or fits certain definitions (of which its author had quite probably never heard). It is classic because of a certain eternal and irrepressible freshness.

— Ezra Pound

Architecture begins where engineering ends.

— Walter Gropius

The Classics

Throughout the process of discovering, selecting and categorizing all the houses that would make up this book about hip and hidden Philadelphia, one thing became clear: The handful of wonderful creations in this first chapter are the ones that laid the groundwork and raised the bar for all the rest. They are the truly iconic works. Like more traditional buildings that scholars and critics generally agree are "classics" – a term too easily and freely applied these days, eroding its meaning and value – the ones on the next few pages are of the highest quality and integrity, possess a certain venerability (the youngest is more than 70 years old), are the work of well-respected architects and provide a standard against which future architects may measure their work, are of enduring interest and are, in their specific ways, definitive. They are all this, and more, and different. For one thing, they are residences; most lists of classic Philadelphia buildings rarely include places designed for families to live in. Beyond that bias, though, they have the capacity to make us stop in wonder and amazement, all the more for our having casually, unintentionally but luckily discovered them. And they have the power to become central, unfrayable and golden threads in the fabric of our memories of the city, and to make us want to see them again (if we can find them again), and to consider them among the best things that the city can offer – the things that make a great city great, or greater. They are the buildings that we can't get out of our minds. They have a "wow" factor that goes beyond the superficial; they touch something within us. They are beautiful, unique expressions that from the beginning did not care that they were different – in fact, that's what they were meant to be. They are esteemed representatives of an informed rebellion that is a key component of hipness. Some may have been shockingly progressive and ill-received when they were constructed – they were confidently out of context and bravely ahead of their time when they were erected or refitted, and they continue to dazzle and surprise to this day. Most have been lovingly maintained, some have been restored. They seem to be alive; they breathe. They are a captured brilliant idea of their time and, somehow, that brilliance has endowed them with a timelessness. Any one of them in a city would be a treasure, an enrichment of the cityscape and the civic culture. Philadelphia has all these, they are undeniable classics, and the city is honored by their presence and legacy.

Victorian and modern at the same time, a station at the junction of a changing world, the Thomas Hockley House is a modest city mansion built in 1875 by the architectural firm of Furness & Hewitt. To describe it as Victorian Eclectic, or even Neo-Grec Second Empire, does not begin to describe its elegance, its eccentricity or its magic. To say that less than twenty years after its construction a new owner made changes to it, and before too much longer it had been broken into apartments, is to tell another sad chapter in the fate of Frank Furness buildings. At least this one is still standing. More like a house/cathedral than just a house, this three-story structure has a mastery of its components that goes beyond mere function and into the realm of art.

There is here a use of decorative elements that one has become familiar with in other Furness buildings, making every aspect a thing of beauty: artistic brickwork and stone carving; minimized columns; a remarkable color palette of dark salmon, pinkish-purplish-gray stone, limestone, accents of black; strong textures; Gothic arches; a jutting bay with brackets. It is a building that, despite the varied materials, seems as though it was carved from a solid block – like a rock-cut temple. It is ornate but not baroque, as are many other Victorians. It is solid but not heavy – in fact, it presents a

remarkably counterintuitive lightness in its masonry, demonstrated especially in the relief over the entrance, which probably weighs a ton, but the flowery design of which makes it feel as if it could fly, or float weightlessly. Timeless and tasteful, like Cary Grant in tails, it is the once and future hip in an ever-changing city, upholding values we cannot afford to forget, and providing an animated yet unassuming presence in its mostly upscale 19th-century neighborhood (a few houses of which are, although uncertainly, also attributed to Furness).

This townhouse underwent an extreme makeover, going from its original Second Empire/Victorian design to the International. Altered in the early 1930s by architect George Howe for attorney and modern art and literature patron (and friend of Ezra Pound and Ernest Hemingway) Maurice Speiser and his wife, Martha, this was a fairly early Modernist design statement for North American inner-city residential taste. This might account for why it hesitantly tries to "fit in" with its neighbors by having the windows remain on the same alignment as the houses next to it, along with suggestions of the same mansard and more traditional cornice. It was revolutionary for its street … but this is Philadelphia, after all. It is, in other words, a modern take on its past and its neighbors' present. Given our knowledge of Howe's work on the Philadelphia Savings Fund Society Building, there is almost something about this house that resembles a mini-skyscraper. A now-classic (but then confrontational) gray and steel-blue painted rowhouse, it was refaced with brick, limestone, and industrial sash. The functional aspects are well designed, and though there is a lack of decoration the whole is of a sleek beauty.

The house is made more horizontal by the grouping and banding of windows, and it is made to seem taller because of the below-grade entrance. This Streamline Moderne step-down is a sort of perverse, subversive critique of the neighbors' step-ups on a street of elegant stair- and social-climbing; in this context, it is a wonderful way to emphasize the entrance, giving it power by taking grandness away from it and humbling it in a decidedly non-humble environment. Plus, the door has a porthole — a big porthole — that not only punctures the facade's unyielding rectangularity but also announces the house's step in the brave new direction of modern reevaluation. Without doubt, this is an outstanding jewel amid a street of posh 19th-century gems, at first stark in comparison with them but smartly drawn and timeless in its simplicity — the very definition of cool (and calm, and collected).

If the Spanish, rather than the Dutch and British, had settled the territory of Philadelphia, the governor of the province would have lived in a place like this. Instead, this truly one-of-a-kind-in-Philadelphia Spanish Revival *palacio* was designed for the man who, with partner Frank Hardart, invented the Automat (the first, in 1902, opened at 818 Chestnut Street). Built in 1929 by architect James P. Metheny (also attributed to A.J. Hall), the Joseph Horn Mansion not only was made to look older than it actually is but also to seem to be in some other place than it actually is. It is a simulacrum of Spanish architecture, like a museum re-creation of a period room, where some real elements are brought in, and then fleshed out with local native materials.

The mansion (now broken into condominiums) looks moss-covered, even though it isn't. It both transports you to another earlier time of courtliness and swashbuckling (decidedly not a Philadelphia time) and looks ahead of its time. In a modern mix of irregular materials, a strategic placement of stone makes it seem as if there is an old facade poking out from a newer stucco job. Huge and faux medieval, it is four houses wide and massive, a solid wall of a building. And yet … you can absolutely walk right by it without noticing it. Unique, quietly confident in its eclectic surroundings of 19th- and 20th-century row-houses, it is nothing like its neighbors. Stone arches, stained glass windows, wrought-iron planters, carved wooden doors — one with iron dog figures, drooping ironwork "barbed wire" and hand-forged hinges — it has the feel of a grand *posada*, where you would expect to see horses tied to a hitching post out front. Standing as interesting "historicity" juxtaposed with the futuristic vision of its owner's ideas about food service, it is Don Diego's place — with the secret exit for Zorro and his steed, Toronado, in the back alley.

This monumental and vibrant place has, strangely, what looks like a protractor etched into the space between windows at the second story. (What it is, really, is a sundial, which is pretty cool in its own right.) The name of this impressive Shingle Style house is "The Anglecot," an 1883 creation for oil-cloth and linoleum manufacturer Charles A. Potter by architect Wilson Eyre, Jr. After many additions and alterations – in 1897, 1898 and 1901 by Eyre; 1902 and 1903 by Charles Cridland; 1906 by John Owens; 1910 and 1916 by Eyre again; 1941, 1956 and 1957 by Paul A. Brosz; and 1981-83 by Greg Woodring, all (and, possibly, others) spanning a hundred years of refinement – it looks, when compared to old photos, like a snazzy stylized version of the original. Handsome, regal and Cotswoldian as it sits angled on its corner site – hence the name – it is extremely graphic and textural with fish-scale cedar shingles, flared chimneys, a brick car court, eyebrow window above the bay, muted color palette, a rich mix of materials and gables outlined in black. Its asymmetry makes it seem rambling. There is something reminiscent of a ship about it, too, with the carved figures flanking the second-story bay window like figureheads at the bow, and as if the captain's quarters were located behind the eyebrow window. Grand, sprawling and manor-like, because of its angling it belongs to no street. This wonderfully attractive house – which, abandoned for nearly a decade in the 1930s and '40s, was used as a nursing home among its various other residential uses, most recently as condominiums – looks as though it should be on a rise overlooking the Sound somewhere instead of its neighboring large 19th- and 20th-century stone estates and contemporaries.

To find one house of this design in Philadelphia is remarkable; to find two is mind-boggling. This pair of mirror-image identical twins, which you might expect to see in a beach community, are on opposite sides and ends of the same block, in an otherwise stone-and-brick neighborhood barely within the city's northern border. They were built in 1936 by architect James A. Nolen, Jr., founder of Nolen & Swinburne, a firm that specialized in commercial architecture. The firm had collaborations with architect Marcel Breuer on two projects in our nation's capital. Although these houses are essentially the same, each has its unique elements. The one on this page sits atop a sloping hill with a series of stairs and landings leading to its entrance. (Just a note: All the homes on this block orient at 90°, or sideways, to the street, so these houses are in step, despite their design differences.) The ceremonial approach adds a bit of grandeur to the place, rising above as it does, making it appear larger than its twin, which sits right at street level. The graded access also gives an opportunity for design-y wrought-iron railings that harken to the period, although they are different from the balustrade railings across the roof terraces of both structures.

Other differences: The house on the previous page is all black and white, while its sibling on this page has turquoise highlights, making it a bit more playful; and the landscaping causes the elevated house to be slightly more hidden, oddly, than the more grounded one. Both are lovely, each in its own way on its own site. They are symmetrical and rectangular, with wraparound casement windows that add to their horizontality. In addition, they possess the pleasing puncuation of porthole windows that hover above a bookend-like pairing of cascading half-circle stairs and their matching inverted eyebrow roofs – the two encasing and delineating the main entry

like a reflection in a pool. Interestingly, both houses have peaked roofs that are barely visible behind the parapet walls that usually indicate flat roofs. As with most Art Deco buildings, they have that smooth, sand-finish stucco that creates a textureless texture that allows the geometry of the architecture to stand proud. It is often said that Philadelphia has one of the richest mixes of housing stock in the country. With these amazing classics of Streamline Moderne, one might wonder if there is any period which is not represented here in this town. Our guess? These two are likely to winter in Miami Beach, where they could go incognito.

Monastery-like, with arches and glimpses of a cloistered courtyard, this residence emerges from a stone retaining wall that surrounds it as if it were carved from a geological formation. It doesn't sit on its land but rather interacts with it and encompasses it in the way of a fortress built into a mountain. Visually, it tempts the viewer to think of a castle with a moat around it, or makes one consider how well the site was used, and how the house becomes a wall that separates house from street. The whole thing says "private" without being unfriendly, giving off a feeling of authority without being oppressive. The front is like a city house that is tall and impenetrable; the back is like a country house that is more closely tied to the grounds — streetside is the palazzo, the garden is the villa, the rear facade resembling an orangery on a large estate. A Norman style dwelling, the Fraley-Howe Residence was built in 1922-23 by the firm of Mellor, Meigs & Howe for architect George Howe's widowed mother.

This distinguished place has a certain stance – an understated class, a regal authority, a manor to the manor born, masterfully unself-conscious in a neighborhood of mostly 19th- and 20th-century stone residences. It is unadorned, yet it fully captures and emanates the beauty in the materials: pink stone with quoining and tan stucco, the foundation story and contiguous wall made up of local schist with quoins acting as gate posts – the tailored-design makes the facade look like it is stitched together by quoining. The materials are solid and eternal, not ostentatious. The soft colors help to hide the structure, giving it an ancient-ruin quality that almost blends into its surroundings. A long vertical arch surrounds and emphasizes windows; there is a medieval sense of limited-access openings, both arched and rectangular, at street level providing brief peeks into private areas. There is a quality about it reminiscent of Hollywood's Golden Age movie-star mansions – one might almost expect to find it crouched back from Sunset Boulevard, with Norma Desmond descending the staircase there.

Old buildings preserve the local culture and identify and create a sense of belonging. In a way, we recycle embodied human resource energy along with material energy. We bring alive the past to be a part of the future, creating important connections through time.
— Vani Bahl

Cities are gentrified by the following types of people in sequence: first the risk-oblivious (artists), then the risk-aware (developers), finally the risk averse (dentists from New Jersey).
— Bill Kraus

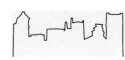

2

Adaptive Reuse

Buildings get reused (except when they get knocked down, often only to have a building with the same function constructed on the same footprint). A store goes out of business; another venture moves into its space. People move from their houses; other people buy those houses and make them their own. Functional fixity – a state of inflexible thinking that causes a person to see only one way of doing something or one unchangeable way of viewing something's use or purpose – is a strong, dominant force in humans, and apparently heightened in those who deal in real estate. Toward the end of the 20th century, however, there was a move to take many old buildings that had outlived the usefulness for which they had been constructed and adapt them for different purposes without noticeable alterations to their facades. Churches, or sections of them, were converted into cafes. Abandoned banks or railway stations became art centers. It might have been an architectural offshoot of the larger reduce-reuse-recycle Green movement, or simply one element of the growing trend toward historic preservation; in a more basic way, it might also have been an acknowledgment of and a capitalizing on high-vacancy (and, thus, more affordable) buildings in the city's core as the center of business and commerce drift-

ed to the west or out of town entirely. With few exceptions, the residential part of adaptive reuse lacked a certain artistry – ironic, since many of the new tenants were artists. For the most part, factories or warehouses with open floor-plans became loft spaces with open floorplans; buildings that no longer suited law and accounting firms had their office layouts remodeled into standard-issue, cookie-cutter apartments with granite counter tops, stainless-steel appliances and Center City views seen through unopenable windows. But then there are others, the hip and hidden ones, with their highly creative adaptations and imaginative reuses, done surely but quietly by ingenious amateurs or visionary architects. These adapted dwellings, unlike their big-budget, high-profile brethren, are to be found for the most part on small streets and alleys, and their choice of reused property can often be deemed "bohemian." In some instances, a few of these residences have been the spark in the evolution of the larger neighborhood around them. For a potentially useful building to be reused is a good thing; for it to be reused well is a smart move; but, for it to be shiningly reused, reflecting personality and spirit, without bragging or compromising its dream – that is a gift.

There was a building on this land as far back as 1745. In 1809, a Baptist church rose on the site, and almost 100 years later it was bought by Byelorussian immigrants and turned into the Neziner Synagogue (Congregation Ahavas Achim Nazin Misach Hoarce, to be precise). And now – since a marvelous 1985 redo by SMGA (Stephen Mark Goldner Associates) – it is condominiums. This unassuming, simple-yet-dignified, country-church-like Greek Revival structure sits back on its sizable lot, cloistered, separated from the street by a fine wrought-iron gate, wide brick courtyard and a towering, aged tree.

With its large, simplified Gothic windows – not stained glass – it is without doubt a house of worship. And yet, though at times it seems to resemble an 18th-century Dutch church, minus the steeple, and at other times that middle-of-the-road grandeur associated with many Greek Orthodox churches, there is something ... French Quarter-ish about its look and feel – all of these placing it out of context in Philadelphia, and especially in its neighborhood of mostly vernacular rowhouses and storefronts. Impressive in its own quiet way, it isn't shy, but doesn't shout. It seems to have a sense of its age and history, and the many kinds of shelter it's been.

This converted and altered former mews stands in contrast to most of its neighbors on an old and narrow alleyway: it is horizontal to the others' verticality, it appears industrial to their residential – and it is not red brick or a facsimile thereof, but a pure, surprising white. By 1948, the original mews had given way to garages, a storage room and plumbing offices, all of which were earmarked for demolition to accommodate a new single-family dwelling. Instead, around 1950, architect Morris J. Rosenthal came up with a two-story design that refaced the original structure in brick, with a garage-door front and a decidedly International-style look. Spare and rectilinear, white facade punched with black doors, what could be a cold-feeling, nearly featureless house is made oddly welcoming by a large and open-armed, espaliered cedar that grounds it. Though somewhat out of place in its context – yet barely visible from the nearby major thoroughfare – this architectural statement is striking in its stark simplicity, boldly confident and beautiful in its own way and on its own terms.

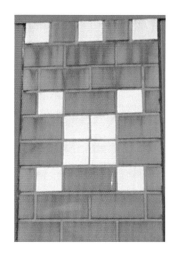

The rest of the street that this small brick building sits on is lined by a quietly attractive and intermittently stylish array of multistory, 19th- and 20th-century structures, some originally commercial, which have been converted into contemporary residences of various forms. In terms of size, this one is the runt of the litter, easily overlooked … literally. It also has a totally different period style. In terms of "hip," it's just right. It looks like a revamped auto-repair shop, but was actually a retail hardware store built in 1946, and, as the area changed, reworked sometime in the 1980s.

It's a quietly cute, playful place, with its asymmetry, the geometric tile work, the flow of glass from sheet to block and the Midwest-style orange brick outlined in blue and detailed in blue and mauve. It is its economies of scale and style that make it seem perfectly rendered and far more impressive than one might think in a casual glance. Like one of those tiny dogs with great body image that doesn't know it's tiny and bravely takes on dogs many times its size, this little building stands tall and merits our attention.

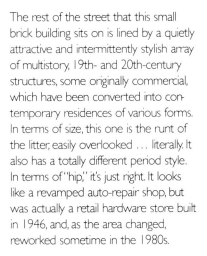

This house will reward walkers who alter their sideways or downward viewing habit and look up. It might even stop them in their tracks when they see the bushy eyebrow of wisteria over the industrial garage door, and the naturalistic shrubbery in right-angled array (lately replacing the pyramidal evergreens pictured here) on this mostly unadorned brick building's rooftop, corralled by a gleaming band of corrugated metal. There is the stylish, woven metal door and wiremesh flower boxes, both a fitting homage to the building's former life as the location of a scrap metal business. In fact, if it weren't for the plant life and a few design touches, it might be easy to misconstrue this basically plain and boxy structure as a still-functioning commercial property. Saved in 1974 from rezoning as a junk yard, the building was purchased in the late 1980s and renovated in the 1990s by architects Amburn/Jarosinski. Hidden in plain sight in a community of 19th- and 20th-century rowhouses, this unostentatious gem is like a penthouse apartment that extends down to the street, without pretense, and with a truly honest use of materials and rich metal textures.

Only the plants hanging in domestic display in a window, or the occasional shadowy movement from within, or sometimes a parked car on the landing, or the recent addition of wrought-iron fencing give away the secret: that this abandoned branch of the Free Library of Philadelphia is now somebody's grand manor house, tucked away on a residential street among rows of 19th-century millworker housing. Despite its new identity, the building would seem to look much the same as it did when it was built in 1909. Architect Lawrence V. Boyd's

Beaux Arts Renaissance Revival design is a mini-estate on a sizable lot defined by a low stone retaining wall; the one-story structure is composed of smooth limestone blocks, ionic columns, keystones and garlands. Above the entrance is a wonderful relief of a heraldic open book amid overflowing cornucopia – certainly designed with the library in mind, but just as appropriate for its current life: a new chapter, brimming with endless possibilities. Though seemingly unaltered by time, it is altered in viewers' minds by knowledge of its current use.

One of the more gratifying and important reuse movements of the past few decades has been the rescue of late 19th-/early 20th-century carriage houses in the city. Some have undergone few and minor alterations to their facades, while others have been enhanced – some with improvement. All are very hip buildings that drew people with a good eye and without functional fixity to call them home. These excellent three are within easy walking distance of each other.

Most unusual, unexpected, charming and mysterious (previous page, top two and lower left) is this three-story, peaked-roof Stuart Revival-style former stable, circa 1910. It has a possible long-forgotten past as a hospital or asylum, a school, or even an athletic club: The eye-catching limestone banding across the Flemish bond brickwork is adorned by a heraldic medallion inscribed with the Latin for "Sound Mind in a Sound Body." Meanwhile, an unassuming, no-nonsense, classy 1880 "city barn" (previous page, right top and bottom) gives a few signs of its intelligence to its narrow street: arched windows, corbelwork cornice, porthole door. It is stoically beautiful, and while its outside hides its artfulness, its altered interior has impressive pedigree – Romaldo Giurgola (of Mitchell/Giurgola Architects) in 1965, Alley Friends Architects in 1982 – and was not only a pioneering residence of that type but also home to a friend of infinite warmth. Finally, on this page, from 1885 – a time when even a grand house's back entrance for horses was better looking than a lot of fronts today – is this two-story, multicolored brick, Victorian Eclectic carriage house with mansard and gable roof sections, a Frank Furness-type sensibility and an air of quiet, formal dignity. Once used as offices, including an architect's, smart and hungry eyes saw it as a perfect residential property, and it began its path to conversion starting with architect Otto Sperr's plans for it as a single-family dwelling in 1993.

The first buildings on this site went up in 1804, but it wasn't until almost three decades later that entrepreneur Joseph Eucinton built three contiguous properties here to house his expanding Quaker Soap and Candle Manufacturing company. The bubbles and wicks are long gone, but the bones of the old structures are detectable (or, perhaps, made to seem that way) within the 1972 redo by architect Adolf DeRoy Mark. It's a clever, even ingenious, melange of old Philadelphia historic and Victorian-meets-Bourbon-Street French. Behind

the brick and stucco facades, with their Main Street U.S.A. gingerbread accessories, through ornate iron gates set in an arched and Belgian-blocked entrance that almost seems like a time-tunnel portal to a lovely past, lies a marvelous courtyard mews of private residences. On the fourth story of the brick portion of the complex is a faux window which masks what looks to be a rooftop deck. This is as much a reinvention as a reuse, a skillful and successful skirting of theme-parkness, and it is as different from its neighbors as it fits right in with them.

As with many of the altered-use buildings in this chapter, this one has seen an incarnation or two. Taller and wider than its neighbors, this was the office/warehouse for Ross Electric Construction in the 1940s and their vehicle garage into the '50s; later, the Inclinator-Elevette company had its offices and stored its elevators here. The building, in a neighborhood of vernacular 19th-century houses, was turned into a single-family dwelling and artist's studio around 2002. Its parapet and casement windows probably date back to commercial alterations done in the '40s. It is hard to tell whether the large cross-buck doors are old or new – the guess would be new, since they don't quite fill the entire opening that was created for trucks, leaving a nice opportunity to do something artistic with glass and moldings. Both plain and fancy, the house exhibits a creative combination of Art Deco facade features and Stick-style doors. painted blue, red and purple, with big red X's that function, in the manner of international signage, much better and with more class than a boringly standard "No Parking" sign.

Considering that it towers over its nearest neighbors by at least one story, considering that it is painted in no fewer than eight colors, considering that it is perhaps Philadelphia's most highly ornamented non-office building … considering all of that, it is astonishing that one can walk almost right past this Italianate gem without noticing it. You have to look up at it, from right in front of it, to get the full impact of its nearly textile-like moldings, its folds and scallops, all remarkably made of cast iron. But don't miss the ground floor's magical decorative facade elements, Try to view it from across the street, and a huge tree blocks your view — which might account, partially, for its near-obscurity. Looking like a giant curbside pipe organ ("The Calliope House," some call it; indeed, it seems steam-powered), standing amidst 18th- to 20th-century rowhouses, it started life in 1851 as Hope Engine Co. No. 17 (it ceased its volunteer-firehouse function in 1871). It was designed by architects Hoxie & Button, who also had a hand in one of the numerous remodelings of the Walnut Street Theatre. Many of the original details, including a carved rendering of the engine-company symbol (a fire-hose nozzle) in a niche at the rooftop, remain, thanks to superior and faithful restoration work. It is exquisite, yet winks at the street with a knowing sense of humor.

The building is very "Philadelphia," in that, despite its cascading ornamentation, it does not overplay its hand. Reimagined, revived and lived in for a time by noted photographer Ray K. Metzker, it is comfortable with its arty identity, especially because there is something so fantastically fairy-tale castle-ish about it – like an item straight out of the Arabian Nights seen through a medieval/Crusades filter. All buildings should be as lucky to get such loving reuse – and more should take themselves as seriously lighthearted as this one does.

Architecture is to make us know and remember who we are.
— Sir Geoffrey Jellicoe

Old buildings are not ours. ... They belong partly to those who built them, and partly to the generations of mankind who are to follow us. ... What we ourselves have built, we are at liberty to throw down. But what other men gave their strength, and wealth and life to accomplish, their right over it does not pass away with their death.
— John Ruskin

3

The Incorporated Past

With a building stock so varied, decorative, decently preserved, historically rich and ripe for redoing, Philadelphia affords the willing and inventive architect, builder or owner the tantalizing opportunity to save and use some details, build over or around others, and so include the old into the new: update the dated, if you will. The old is left as a counterpoint to the new, or, perhaps, to lend the new a kind of acceptance gained from association with the old's acquired "street cred." Maybe leaving some of the old has to do with generating a sense of continuity and honesty … or, in some cases, it is simply an unwillingness or inability to choose one over the other: stymied compromise as design feature. The attitude is both respectful and adventuresome, a fence-sitting stance that allows the house to live graciously in both worlds and to be individualistic in its duality. As a kind of archeological layering, the best and most knowing of these inclusive-minded dwellings present a sort of pentimento, in which the original or older details seem to be resurfacing from under the "overpainted" facades. Sometimes it's just the opposite: the new elements seem literally to be erupting from within the old, like the sprouting of fresh ideas in solid form. There is usually no question as to which parts came before and which came after, but, especially in the more artful and adroit creations — as in this chapter — one time-specific element does not dominate the other but, in fact, aids the other in being pertinent in the current scheme of things. Some purists might consider such alterations a kind of misguided science creating Frankenstein's monsters, but these selections have a unique charm based on their unorthodox and intelligent blending of parts, not for the goal of historical consistency but, rather, for design effect and effective integration. In small scale, these homes are parables of Philadelphia's architectural, social and economic ebb and flow, as well as its citizens' tug of loyalty between the past and future.

Unconventional, snazzy, Art Deco with an attitude – this building is a lovely little nonconformist surprise on an otherwise nondescript block of 19th-century rowhouses. Built around 1925, most likely as an apartment building or commercial property, it retains its interesting stepped brick patterns. There is a more recently applied stainless steel eyebrow portico with its vertical elements acting as columns, enhanced by glass block, a series of transom windows, and a purple door – all filling the void of the original display area where the storefront window might have been. It nicely preserves original elements, while stylizing others (the painted stepped brick string course is one example). Probably in the 1980s much of the lower portion was postmodernized, which works quite effectively in bringing the brickwork to the ground, like a cascade of succeeding design generations. Squint your eyes, forget its history, and it looks like a Native American headdress gone all geometric. A bold face on the street, it is both sophisticated and unlikely, yet plays well with its neighbors.

Don't try pigeonholing the great Philadelphia architect Frank Weise. On the one hand, he could create as eye-blinkingly original a home as one could imagine (see *Unique, No Comparables*); on the other – and right next door – he could redo a building and make one wonder if anything had even been done to change it. (He performed the same sort of architectural prestidigitation on the renovated Head House Square, in Society Hill.) In fact, this was two two-story Italianate stables from around 1860, converted between 1991 and 1993 into one large complex with a third-story penthouse and visible roof deck. What's old here, and what's new? There is a trueness to the details that makes it hard to tell, and the improvements lend a more ancient air to the facade. Arched, shuttered windows with grates; steel lintels; bracketed wood cornice – are they from the 19th century or the 20th? Is it a place that's aged well, or been reborn? The tongue-and-groove doors and exterior wainscoting definitely look old, but almost certainly they are not, and the ironwork looks almost medieval. It is superior work carefully done to keep original things while adding new things made to look old. In its serious way it's a spirited building, all about grids, with many openings, many shapes, all tied together with great finesse, beautifully, cleanly … and modestly.

Carved out of the abandoned, seven-building carcass of the old Capital Meats packing plant (closed in 1989), this large structure retains its commercial bones. But architect Tim McDonald has made it more than just another residential loft-space rehab in the city – he's turned it into a rollicking Cubist billboard for a neighborhood in the ascendancy. By doing so, in 2000-2002, he defined – within the context of 19th-century worker houses and other early-20th-century commercial properties – the neighborhood's newfound flair for incorporating the old with the avant. Still intact is part of the original brick facade with its ghostly signage, but round the corner and it is a new world, an amalgam of corrugated metal, boxy primary-color balconies (which might show where fire-escape stairs once were), square protruding flanged windows, tubular metal, steel entries and treads.

The totality is similar, in size and material, to a ship's hull. This unusual assemblage of disparate elements risked being an incoherent hodge-podge of metal frameworks and structures, but the result is, instead, elegant and attractive, compelling in its individuality – a sculptural patch-work quilt, faceted and geometric. In this profusion of rectilinear shapes and textures, the metalwork takes a flat facade and makes it three-dimensional and contempo-rary. The metal additions are heavy but the property is large and, because of its vast site, seems prac-tically hidden from many vantage points. Reminiscent of a Northern European factory, barracks or prison, this advertisement for change faces away from its past, reflecting the new, shinier future. Both worlds coexist, the conver-gence of the extant and the embel-lishment tied together by design, and it works.

An eclectic corner redo of a commercial property into residential, in a neighborhood of 19th-century rowhouses, this place has a mixed-bag history of alterations. In 1940, it was a neighborhood grocery store with an electric Coca-Cola sign hanging out front. Times and neighborhoods change, and, by 1972, it was vacant. Then the corner-store entry was bricked up to create a single-family dwelling. In 1985, archi-tect Alvin Holm was called in by a new owner to redesign the interi-ors, and he provided some direction for facade renovation, as well. The exterior changes are modest in scope, embracing what was there, respecting the original and embel-lishing it with something unique – a kind of improvisational vernacular. The front door resembles an entry salvaged from an Art Nouveau bank, with filigree and leaded glass. Nearly encased by the walls of the closed-up old commercial entry, the original faceted corner column stands out as a historically resonant yet completely self-sustaining design element that is like a remnant of an arabesqued archway. It would cer-tainly have been easier to eliminate the column, but instead it is pre-served and showcased to excellent artistic effect. There is a classical quality to the articulation of the facade, a rusticated scoring of the almost adobe-like stucco, radiating from an all-important arched win-dow and transitioning into the old brick at the second-floor window-sill level. The palette is pink and sand-colored, with a reflective quali-ty, and there is a distinct feel of a blending of European and Middle Eastern sensibilities. It is an individu-alistic, unduplicatable house, easily overlooked and underappreciated.

This place seems to have always had a style – somewhat like a working-class palazzo in Florence – distinct from the surrounding 19th-century rowhouses and storefronts. It's been a corner store, then a two-family residence with ground-level barbershop, later a mostly vacant building with day-care center. It was made completely residential in 1991. In 1996, architect Ralph C. Fey designed exterior changes. The echoes of classical styles created in newer materials on the ground floor add to an already striking original facade with three stories of banded pilasters – touches of Neoclassicism – resulting in an attractive merging of old and new. At street level there is a raised foundation line with a limestone ledge, removing it from the street but giving something back, as well. The openings may reference original ones, but are now replaced by decorative niches. Scoring in the brick across the first story relates to the pilasters and provides a horizontal counterbalance to the verticality of the building. The central arch and cut-glass windows resemble a restored old Roman wine cellar. It all blends, avoiding a theme-park kitsch or stylistic mishmash.

Talk about multiple personalities. Built in 1873 by James McAleer (McAleer & Burkmire), a mason and builder, as his own single-family dwelling, this structure became a rooming house near the turn of the century, a retail outlet for a bottler before Prohibition, a barroom in the 1930s, a Chinese takeout, another tavern that for some reason was made to look like a log cabin and, in the 1960s, the office of a plumbing and heating contractor. Coming full circle, it is a house once again. Its Victorian structure is still visible, but period architectural detail, apart from the roof, is long gone in all the various changes. In the process of becoming residential again – and thoroughly (and idiosyncratically) personalized by new owners – the entrance was altered in 1992 by landscape architect Julie Regnier, resulting in a Streamline Moderne portal, a swath of tropical-style plants and, imbedded in the cement, geometric tile "rugs" on entry landings.

The metal work, on the curved stucco entry walls (anodyzed aluminum acting as design stripes, or bumpers) and collaged driveway gate, is unique. The entire place – brick to Wissahickon schist to stucco – is an eclectic grouping of design periods: Greek Revival-influenced cornice returns, 1920s casement windows, post-war '40s front door with South Philly-ish interlocking circular windows turned upright, retro '60s fiberglass awnings. It is a mixed metaphor that retains its past as it looks at its present, coming together in an abridged history of Philadelphia housing. On a corner of an out-of-the-way, hard-surface neighborhood, it is a kind of oasis, a caravanserai, singular among otherwise stripped-down Victorians and early 20th-century rowhouses. A blocky building, shaped like a Monopoly hotel piece (but with a ton of windows), a mass of geometric solids softened by playful and personalized elements, circles and rounded edges, and greenery – it is what it is: one big assembled work of art.

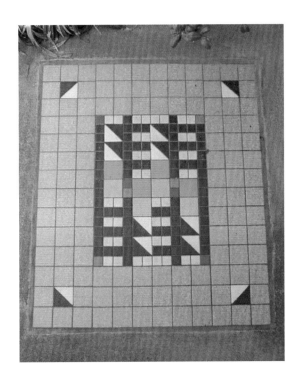

Sometimes hip can mean having spunk, and this residence has it. Happily rounded in a rectangular world, asymmetrical in an 18th- and 19th-century neighborhood of symmetry, this Art Deco structure is a narrow, curved-corner brick building that might have been built as a store in the early 1930s. (The photos on this page show it as we first saw it; on the next page is how it appears today, after a recent major overhaul.) Looking a little like a turret that fell off another building, giving it echoes of castleness, at the same time it also has resonances of warehouse/industrial, like Coca-Cola bottling plants or telephone company buildings, erected in a Moderne style, that were scattered throughout cities at that time. It has a shape unique in any neighborhood but a real anomaly on this street of post-Revolutionary "colonial atmosphere." Very quietly subversive, graceful and unassuming, it is a delight that is thoroughly out of context, and yet it somehow recedes into the background. Providing a service to a densely built street, it opens the corner and the intersection not only with its curvy shape and diminutive size but also because of its large windows (formerly glass block) and incised pattern of horizontal lines (its only real decorative element). On such a small building, the banding enhances its size but reduces its mass; in addition, the large curved windows almost make it disappear. Because this house is of its time there is a kind of "datedness" about it, making it appear older than some of the surrounding buildings that *are* older; still, it is futuristic – that kind of "used future" seen in interesting science-fiction films.

That being said about its old self, here is its new revised self ready for the 21st century. Used for storage in the late 1930s, it was renovated into an office and apartments in 1940 by architect J. Fletcher Street, and that became its fate for sixty-five years. In 2005 it was redesigned as two single family dwellings with an added third story, front and rear nautical-railed decks, new casement windows and plain doors. It is a respectful pairing of the familiarly old and livably new. Jutting angles of the metal-clad third story have a similar playful nod to the sweet and friendly stature of the "given," not overpowering it but, rather, topping it off like a new coif. The railings pick up the lines of the building, both its angles and curves, and its incised brick pattern. Although the glass block will be missed a little, there is now a more serviceable window configuration and still plenty of horizontals with the additional verticals, resulting in a graphically pleasing interface. It is the little turret that could, and someone did a nice job of making it live again, as it approaches its first hundred years.

Can anything make a city house more luxurious than the addition of a garden entrance? This modernized 19th-century rowhouse has a set-back garden (and any setback in the city that is not created for off-street car parking is rare and welcome, indeed) and an entry addition in the adjacent lot. Rehabilitated and rebuilt circa 1974 by architects John Lloyd & Associates, the structure is a large residence that uses ceramic tile as a graphic-design motif for tying all the various parts together, in spite of the fact that some of those parts are older and original while others are much newer. Like tailored stitching, brown glazed tile surrounds and outlines every window and door.

The tile acts, in a way, as a replacement for wood trim; it is used as a kind of wainscoting or cummerbund spanning the lower foundation and continuing across the garden wall, giving an informal formality to the structure. There is a Spanish/Mediterranean feel to the color, the tile, the large entrance arch, the paneled door, the courtyard, the wrought-iron light fixtures. The garden wall has a more contemporary custom-metal trellis and center entry gate, but both have a graphic style that works with the whole. An ingenious blending of old and new in a consistent simplification and systemization, the re-designers applied a grid and patterning that retained and renovated without removing or radically changing the past. Situated in an eclectic block, with rowhouses from 1807 to more modern times, this consciously, confidently well-designed dwelling is subtle, smart and individual.

With an unabashed sales pitch, the building known as "Venez Voir" ("Come See") seems like something you'd find in Paris in the 1920s, perhaps left from the Exposition d'Arts Moderne et Decoratifs. A modernized 1897 Queen Anne townhouse, its facade alteration looks not only authentically French but designed from the ground up to be that way. The "tell" comes when one looks more closely at the upper stories, camouflaged by being "grayed out" – flattened and neutralized by dark paint. Though not entirely negated, the details of old and new blend nicely, and the old looks a bit French itself with the ironwork balcony above the bay. Refaced at street level in the 1930s as a parfumerie that disappeared by 1949, it was then converted into an architect's office and single-family dwelling by former Mellor, Meigs & Howe architect Edward H. Wigham.

The new front expresses that fascinating crossover from Art Nouveau to Art Deco (with touches of Egyptian). Curved X's top an arched window; wrought-iron grilles and the door grate radiate wavy lines and a motif of ravens; the door sits beneath a porthole and is crowned by arabesqued molding; and the reliefs of ravens repeat above the pilasters as capitals. The design – an extremely rich use of materials and textures, sensual, exotic and mysteriously seductive – beckons like a thinly veiled harem girl, drawing us toward the now-curtained window. The entrance suggests the face of a harlequin, mouth open wide, as at the doorway to a funhouse, which – though graceful and refined – it is.

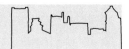

I know that one should resist the impulse to anthropomorphize, but town houses have a presence and a civility missing from more monolithic forms of residential real estate, particularly high-rise apartment buildings. ... a house may guard the mystery of its inner life, but its face invites us to imagine that it has one.

— **Judith Thurman**, *The New Yorker*, December 1, 2003

The beautiful is as useful as the useful ... and perhaps more so.

— **Victor Hugo**

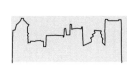

4

Facelift

While some of the chapters in this book easily could be titled or subtitled "The Innovators," the buildings in this section might more aptly be labeled "The Renovators." This is no disparagement in any way – no ghetto-izing of them as second-class citizens – for the vision, artistry and mastery involved here to reface existing properties is as rich and full (and hip) as any "from scratch" creations. In fact, it might perhaps be more intricate and difficult to do this reworking than to start fresh. Most are major undertakings (or is it "overtakings"?) that might be termed reconstructive surgery. The point, it seems apparent, is to mask the past or, maybe, to create a past that didn't exist. The reasons are numerous, including demands of the housing market, or wanting to hide the evidence of two or more properties having been combined into one, or to rescue a house victimized by age and neglect; in other instances, it's to satisfy a desire to embellish or simplify, or, perhaps, to "modernize." What distinguishes a facelift house from one that incorporates the past (as in the previous chapter) is a matter of the degree of change. The alteration is more complete in facelift houses, a kind of makeover rather than just a prettying-up. And even though it isn't a measured amount of work involved, it is the final product and how different it has become that is the true measure. Indeed,

the impulse to make the dwellings look more new than old, or to change them beyond recognition – to create a narrative or theme that doesn't seem to relate to neighboring houses – might strike purists and other architecture-philes as something close to criminal. It certainly is controversial, and goes against much of the historic-preservation movement of recent years. It is also the complete reverse of the now-popular "facadectomy" – or, as some call the trend, "facadomy" – in which all parts of old buildings are removed and replaced except for their aged facades, leaving a "veneer of history"; here, it is the facade that is replaced, applying a veneer of currency. But whatever the level of anger or dismay, it is a fact that these alterations occur, and that their inclusion here is to point out those that are extremely successful, those that are undeniable improvements and others that are works of art built upon an undistinguished, inappropriate or even crumbling structure. They all exhibit a strong sense of style. One can imagine that to an architect or builder of quality each of these was simply too hip a project to avoid, too exciting a challenge, an inventive – even landmark – drawing-board idea that screamed for realization. What we are given, in the end, is a house that has a new look and a fresh start by someone who cared about it.

Long before the recent fascination with the Mission look, this circa 1860 house was redone, around 1940, in a Mediterranean/Spanish Revival style (although it retained much of the old superstructure, most notably window placement). Like the East Coast version of Hearst Castle, there is an authenticity in its design, a completed vision wherein every detail adds to the whole. It makes an amazing statement as a convincing recreation of a Spanish hacienda in a city that was very un-Spanish, indeed, in most other respects. This house is a treasure trove of hipness because it is done to the max, but skirts being cute or campy by being perfectly realized. Known as the Birnbaum Residence, it is a sensual building, wearing a rich array of different material textures: clay-colored stucco and tile coping with arches, terra cotta roof-tile hoods over windows, lattice, a heavy paneled door with forged hardware, projecting vigas, columns and funnel-shaped balconies, all topped by a kind of Spanish mansard. Because of its height and enhanced verticality it is the El Greco of city houses, but that doesn't reflect on its clarity of vision. Amid the surrounding brick 19th-century rowhouses it stands out for its earnestness in attempting a singular look, beautifully present in every time and place.

Looking like a mini-me of George Howe's Maurice Speiser House (see *The Classics*), this unassuming, elegant International/Moderne rowhouse could easily be missed in its 19th-century neighborhood consisting mostly of Italianate, Jacobean Revival or Second Empire homes. It is an alteration of a circa 1870 original building that became vacant in 1932. Facade changes, by architect D. Medoff, in 1938, were made to create a doctor's office and single-family dwelling. Additional changes were made in 1962, also for shopfront and dwelling. The spare limestone facade is pierced by gridded casement windows and a five-light door, and complemented by quirky purple trim. The facade acts as a container for openings, and the scoring around them adds even more to the modern penchant for horizontality, a breaking away from the verticality of most urban rowhouses. This building achieves correctness and balance with minimal effort, retaining a strong design – using geometry and simplicity instead of ornamentation – that still works as a subtle, stylish addition to the streetscape. It is a flat and linear graphic rendering, a sketch for a house that is perfect the way it is.

This Moderne townhouse would appear to be stranded in a sea of 19th-century Second Empire and Victorian houses, all from about 1879. But, actually, it perfectly belongs because, once, it was one of them. It is a 1920s/1930s-style alteration for Dr. T. William Sunderman by Harry Sternfeld, one of the city's great unsung architects, who worked with Paul Cret and who built what is now the Art Institute of Philadelphia – formerly the WCAU studios – on the 1600 block of Chestnut Street, as well as landmark city projects like the Benjamin Franklin Parkway and the Ninth and Market Streets Post Office. At the time it must have been a kind of revolutionary house on this block, and yet it is beautifully understated when seen through today's eyes. It is hard to imagine that it was converted, in 1948, from housing six doctors' offices to a one-family dwelling. Five years after that, it became a catering business and three apartments. In 1976, architect Thomas McHugh turned it into a two-family house.

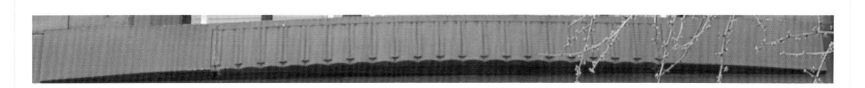

This structure's very vertical facade is made horizontal by a symmetrical plan and massing, typical of Art Deco, with double staircases, paired and separated doors and streamlined ironwork. Linearity and grids (repeated in windows and doors) are superimposed over a flat incised surface and add dimension and depth to the building, while the front steps, turned 90 degrees and divided into a matched set, provide some distance from the street. The color, a beautiful rich chocolate-brown, gives the facade a soft texture that recedes and at the same time emphasizes the designwork details: faceted glass, hardwood, wrought-iron sconces and railings, porthole windows – all black outlines drawn on the burnt umber canvas. New owners have removed the lovely brown from the first floor face, uncovering a terrazzo-textured cementitious material that is subtler in its effect and more original to its design. A curved sill, suggestive of an eyebrow, signals the transition from redesigned to original facade. Most delightful, the extravagant though subtly layered design alteration holds its own among grand Victorians, crossing through the 20th century and beyond into the future.

Sometimes there is a property that takes your breath away because it is so ideally presented. This handsome redo of two rowhouses made into one is stylish and grandly understated but very well-stated. Its refinement is much like a bit of tony London or Washington's Embassy Row. It has a classic simplicity and symmetry, with an attractive little shrub hedge across its front acting as a perfectly trimmed mustache on a dapper gentleman. Stately and formal in a neighborhood of 19th-century brownstones, this house is Fred Astaire in a group of middle-aged men. The original 1857 buildings were altered in 1998 by stuccoing and scoring the facade and replacing windows with cobalt blue casements. A change of the entrance from one side of the building to the other allows the house to be remarkably wide open and yet keep its secrets; the number of windows provides a kind of reflective camouflage in an extremely open site. Not hidden, exactly, but subtly present, classy and even offbeat, the face that this house reveals is one that might be expected to be seen at the waterfront because of its generous panoramic views and a nautical-themed rooftop deck, complete with rope-like railings. This house exudes a contentment that says, "I'm not showy, I've got style."

As cool, blonde and stylishly quiet as Tippi Hedren in Hitchcock's *The Birds*, this modernized townhouse, like the topiary that bookend its entrance, is controlled and contained. The design is clean, solid, flat, spare and sleek, and quite commanding. A vacant shell among 18th- and 19th-century residences in 1986, the place was completely overhauled and renovated by the firm of Amburn/Jarosinski with a facelift of beige/tan brick (a sly, homogeneity-smashing way of keeping within that area's surface-material restrictions, yet giving it a modern, almost stucco-looking facade), casement sash and a repeated "T" design (rightside up, upside down) on the facade, giving it detail without details. The limestone T's make it seem wider than it is by emphasizing the horizontality of the otherwise tall, narrow structure; T's are repeated in windows and in door design, creating both positive and negative T's. Perhaps "T" stands for topiary, an essential element in the mix, as it adds something organic, yet geometricized; since topiary tends to be associated with formal, wealthy estates, it lends an air of class and money to this house, yet it is so out of context on a city street that it becomes a point of humor or whimsy – like two poodles, instead of two lions, at the gate.

These fraternal-twin properties both have lion heads; one house, however, has been made to look contemporary while the other displays traditional/classic touches. Both were vacant in 1988, when new fronts were added. One has vertical wood slats (a kind of awning/spandrel effect) connecting all three stories of windows into one vertical ribbon; it also has painted gray banding across the lower facade (an abstracted nod to the stone foundation courses one sees in older buildings all over town) that ties in the windows to the contemporary flush door, with its chrome hardware, and to a modern porch light. The other house is a bit more referential to the past with more traditional windows topped by lunettes, a panel door with brass hardware and a brass porch light. Each has applied house numbers that fit its "period." They are mid-19th-century rowhouses with simplified stuccoed facades and exaggerated dentil molding cornices. A unique update, they are individualized expression in an otherwise conformist setting. They are hip because they play with the form, because they take artistic chances and because they cleverly use the vernacular and the materials to both update and refer. Certainly, there are some theatrics going on here — the two together are like a stage set with backdrop and props creating a world in which one can walk from one century to the next in one step.

Often hip can be a contextual issue, as when one happens upon a Miami-suburban-style house in a colonial neighborhood. This is not an alteration of the original colonial building – that was condemned and torn down in 1939. The lot stayed vacant for more than a year, after which a hardware store was built. In 1964, the store, then vacant, was converted into a single-family dwelling by architect Louis Sauer. Further exterior changes were made in 1987. This unique corner house, now a pale green stucco with white trim that would fit nicely into any beach community, is a box with spare and select decorative touches: porthole door, minimal x-patterned ironwork, glass block, clean lines. It has an odd shape and size, compared to other houses, a bit startling in its environment, and it seems to have more of a relationship with a houseboat than a city house. Its design seems more to refer to the year that the original structure disappeared than when the new one was built. Hidden on a tiny street with 18th-century houses and some garages, this house acknowledges a modernism based on an industrial aesthetic, using atypical elments for residential purposes, acknowledging its commercial roots: intelligent design that transforms one thing into another in a stylish way.

Like a city house in Japan, this plain beauty has all the style of simplicity with just the right complement of nature. A calming and delightful respite from the surrounding 19th-century vernacular housing on a tiny street, this structure could perhaps be vernacular in 19th-century Kyoto. Kind of a blank canvas of masonry, detailed with an Asian sensibility and landscaping, this extra-broad facade alteration was done in 1984 by architect James Oleg Kruhly.

Unified by a stuccoed facade, gridded windows, heavy and mysterious zen-monastery wooden door below a bracketed copper roof or awning, forged hardware and lantern, and a basic slab slate porch, this townhouse is both rustic and urban at the same time. Happening upon this building on a city street is like finding a teahouse while hiking through a town or park outside Tokyo. Its man-made symmetry has a little natural-material asymmetry thrown in for good measure.

This techno-townhouse was born, as were its late-Federal neighbors, between 1840 and 1859. A vacant single-family, it was redesigned in 1962 by architect David Williams, and later altered and elaborated by architect Christopher Beardsley in 2002-03. The use of corrugated metal creates an elegant industrial style without historical pretense. Simplified, modernized and minimalized, all original references and details are gone; the structure is unadorned other than by asymmetrical design and the beautiful contrasting colors of moss green and silver. It has a commercial feel: it could be a doctor's office, or a takeout window for a foodery of some sort. It is, nevertheless, straightforward and unabashed in its spareness and no-nonsense beauty, exuding a warmth that comes, surprisingly, out of such cool materials. There is the aesthetic of Airstream about it – as if the front could slide open or flip up on a hinge to integrate with its chosen campsite: the street. Seeming more earthbound and urban than its neighbors, the building appears lower to the ground than the surrounding architecture, and more connected. The corrugated metal, in its small area of coverage, creates a kind of brick-like linear texture on an otherwise smooth facade. Some buildings work hard to have a little character using lots of applied architectural stuff, but this one has a judicious amount of applied stuff and ample amounts of character.

Can a building be a sort of *trompe l'oeil*? This British-looking facade plays off the suggestion that it could very well be a finely restored pre-Revolutionary carriage house, or something to do with the colonial governor. It isn't. In its way, it seems more historically original – authentic – than the authentic 19th-century originals around it. It is, however, postmodern. Its deceptive diminutive size makes the viewer think it is something reclaimed, but certainly not the commercial building/warehouse, built circa 1920, that it started out life as. The conversion to residential and a new facade occurred in 1997-98, designed by Nelson and Associates, utilizing generic transcultural references: 18th-century Flemish-bond brick, 20th-century parapet roof line adorned with terra cotta reliefs, limestone Doric column, wrought-iron wagon-wheel motif grating across windows, paneled door with brass hardware. Petite, understated, tasteful and – though frozen in the look of a time, but not actually of that time – timeless.

Like a diner designed by Mondrian, a modern homage to an industrial aesthetic, this beautiful find sits contentedly on an otherwise obscure, hard-to-find, recently rediscovered and rehabilitated service alley sparsely populated by 19th- and 20th-century rowhouses. A tiny place, it has an official name, though: "House for Two." In 1963 its three stories became two; in 2000, what remained was given this high-style rehab by architect Christopher Beardsley. A simple box, it is made spectacular and endearing by the addition of simple things, like the windows — colorful, modern, industrial fenestration which can make the building appear cross-eyed when the pink inner frames are repositioned — or the cute "mouth" that the door seems to display in an anthropomorphic/cartoonish way. The dynamism of the corrugated aluminum that alters direction, giving asymmetry to a fairly blockish thing, makes for a wonderfully playful yet formal facade. Because it's on a street hardly anybody goes down or even knows exists, it is a pioneering effort — a style outpost designed and built with the knowledge that few would ever see it. In that way, it is a futuristic valentine waiting to be opened and adored. Until then, it's the brave little toaster.

Hip is the sophistication of the wise primitive in a giant jungle.
— Norman Mailer

A modern, harmonic and lively architecture is the visible sign of an authentic democracy.
— Walter Gropius

5

Pioneers

These mostly architect-designed homes show what their creators were thinking about the direction of their craft at the time the buildings went up. As noteworthy indicators of transformative moments in the architectural historical continuum, they might reflect ideology based on theroretical thought, cultural and social forces of change, design ideas or personal credos. The architects moved on to other ideas; the buildings have stayed in their time, snapshots of those days of future past – influential examples of recent modern history, and still hip after all these years. They signaled a progressive attitude in building, and they continue to act as those signposts even in the rearview mirror. They are like favorite high-style designer clothes that we bought seasons back but still wear unselfconsciously and with aplomb: they aren't today's style, but they are never out of style, and every once in a while they are rewarded by becoming the objects of great adoration for their authenticity, their honest and true design sense, and

their continued and happy survival and integrity in a constantly changing and alteration-happy world. Besides, they fit so well, and feel so comfy. Unlike the buffed and pristine colonial houses one finds in the more touristy and photogenic parts of town, these residences are not frozen in amber, or meant to look like museum-quality displays. The fact is, they are far more individualistic statements and often more challenging to encounter and ponder than the "historical" development houses that receive all the usual attention. At least one of the houses that follow has gotten a substantial revamp, and – who knows? – perhaps others are being eyed for the same. But these are tough places with strongly held and hard-to-alter identities that surely fought enough style wars and zoning battles to get themselves built in conservative surroundings in the first place; like pioneers of old, they made the journey early, staked their turf, put down roots and aren't going anywhere.

Some houses, like this one, can retain the pioneering spirit even in the face of change. When it was first photographed for this book it was as you see it on this page. A return visit showed it to be undergoing substantial renovations, altering its facade, bestowing on it a more rounded and streamlined Moderne-ish look. The alterations complete, pictured on the opposite page, it is happily still recognizable. The Charles H. Woodward House, now and as it was for most of its 70-plus years, is a hybrid: a cross (according to city documents) between Norman and International styles. It plays with both forms, the traditional (in the way of an English country home) as well as the modern, and combines them successfully. Built in 1938-39 by architect Kenneth M. Day (son of famed Philadelphia architect Frank Miles Day) for Woodward – a lawyer and philan-thropist who, through inheritance of Pennsylvania Railroad money and one-half the rental properties in the neighborhood, was once called "the last de facto feudal lord of Chestnut Hill" – this white, massive, rectilinear facade has horizontal banding of casement windows and narrow stone sills with a hipped roof, an overhanging center bay and walled courtyard. When constructed it was more modern than its neighbors, exhibiting very little in the way of decoration except for elaborate ironwork at the entrance and an interesting pairing of genuine vs. faux espaliers, both of which now seem to be removed in the renovation. A transitional house, living in both worlds (typical of Day's later work), beholden to the past while cleverly incorporating visions of the future in a traditionalist neighborhood of early 20th-century mini-estates, this structure retains its "houseness," yet breaks away from predictability or high-tone stodginess.

The house is set back, but very much out front as it postures aggressively on its site. A bit boxy, yet fluid, it is assertive in a modern way, yet very stately in a conventional sense. Compared to some of its more newly-built neighbors, it has not been, for quite some time, as shocking as it must have been in the early 1940s; in 21st-century eyes, it seems even somewhat sedate and orthodox. But it has retained a hipness of character that has carried through its intelligent design and, even with alterations, will continue to do so. The visible changes end up being not so visible. The courtyard wall has been raised and enclosed, keeping the line of the old wall by extending its height with a horizontal band of referential glass block. The filigree ironwork at the entry is gone and a plain extra-tall door mimics the windows above. A new balcony juts out from one flank and looks as if it was always there. The best update of all, though, is the new fence, a replacement for a former debasing and undeserved stockade type – the new stylish aluminum or stainless-steel version has wide panels spaced like teeth that, again, reflect the shapes and lines of the vertical windows. An excellent and respectful redo by architect John Di Benedetto in 2005-06; a pioneering effort in improving a classic house for the next century.

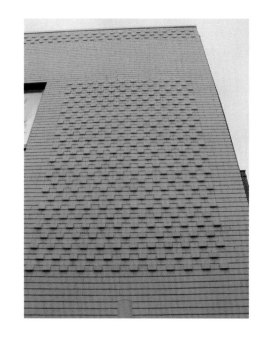

Textural and tactile, this unique house is like a weaving or a Berber rug – a brick tapestry. With a new brick-front addition to an existing photographer's shop and garage, it was updated circa 1961 for the purpose of converting it into a single-family dwelling – a stylish city abode with parking that looks a little like a school of design sitting in among a now mostly residential block of converted carriage houses. The architect, A. Jacobson & Sons, created an International/Modern facade with a kind of minimalism – white painted brick, stepped brick cornice, brick relief detail as decorative mural, vertical window/entrance with porthole door, light green trim. A subtle yet strong design. Later renovations were undertaken in 1988 by Brawer & Hauptman, Architects. The facade, divided into two side-by-side rectangular, vertical blocks, is different on each side: one is Mondrian-ish glass and solids, spaces made up of lines and rectangular shapes; the other is solid brick with a raised pattern above a garage door. The protruding "relief" acts as scales, or tufts, with the overall texture seeming almost like another window – a solid window. A formal design, the brickwork gives the facade dimension, depth and decoration. Despite the date of its refacing, the place has the look and feel of being older – almost 1920s Bauhaus – and its spareness and economy of both materials and decorative elements make for no wasted gesture, a place for everything, everything in its place. It is far friendlier than you would think it could be, and gives the impression of being softer than it is possible to be, but that is part of its dazzling simplicity and exceptional artfulness.

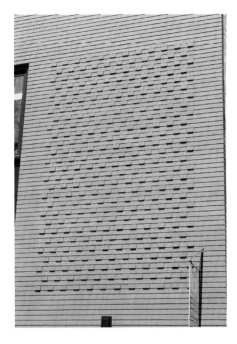

Enter a new era: A revisit to the site somewhat after the photographs on the previous page were taken revealed a changed building. After the initial shock, the question was: Are we still talking about the same house? Also, let it be noted that something else had changed: the windows above the door are no longer divided vertically, removing some of the Mondrian-esque flourishes of line. Also, the choice of black solidifies the window grouping into a block and flattens what had been more varied and design-y and stylized, even shadow-enhanced. The applied red color may be an attempt to disguise what this special place is by making it match its brick sidewalls and bringing it into conformity with its neighbors. But it is the bones of its design that makes it special, and, despite being tampered with, it is still hip, and now even more hidden.

On a busy street, with not much in the way of sidewalk, behind a tall, characterless, standard-issue stockade fence and a wall of trees – in a neighborhood of early 20th-century stone houses trying to look like 19th-century British estates – hunkers, as if hiding from paparazzi, this star-power 1964-65 residence built by architect Thomas A. Todd to be his own home. The L-shaped block and stucco structure, the large band of International-style clerestory windows trimmed in purple (repainted, since these photos, a soft green), the metal standing-seam roof – all make this residence look like a factory in some European woods. Rustic in its setting yet modern in its approach, it is all angles and planes. Tucked away on a wooded lot but outstanding in its context, it is a modern manor, castlelike, fortresslike, even bunkerlike. The house peers out over the fence, almost literally – the row of horizontal windows is like a periscope looking up and out; one might even imagine it as machine-gun emplacements. Considering the time when it was built, there is also something very "hippie-ish" about the place that the seemingly haphazard arrangement of space suggests. The layout is like a play on grouped or clustered contemporary townhouses, with some sections turned sideways, others to the front or the back. One feels something cubist, constructivist or maybe deconstructivist about it, with its sharp-edged angles and faceted blocks – as if the pieces of an old French manor, along with its barn, were disassembled, shaken up in a bag, and reconstituted in a different configuration. Despite its relative newness, it has classic qualities that are timeless, such as its now well-aged stucco walls, its close relationship to the road and its vine-covered tower, not to mention the forecourt entry. The Todd House has an individualism that was engaging, if not startling, back then, and performs the same act today.

This wide residence – built not only in the space of two former townhouses but incorporating the structure of a mattress warehouse that replaced them – was designed in 1976 by architect Alden Blyth, then of Baker, Rothschild, Horn & Blyth. An arrangement of shapes and colors, it could have been planned using a set of Colorforms, but in muted hues. There is no symmetry on the facade other than the twin garage doors, yet there is a balance of elements that relieves the potentially heavy intrusiveness of such a large swath of "dead space" on a city street. The antithesis of a vertical city house in every respect, its facade is more akin in structure to an Egyptian pylon, the entrance being a narrow recess in a monumental wall that is relieved only at the top by a clerestory that gives the illusion of the temple behind the gate. It has a nice mix of materials and textures – colored stucco, brick (reds and grays, which refer to the neighborhood), painted wood, a frame of vertical striping that repeats in the entry. As has been said of paintings of the Classic Modernist or Constructivist styles, which this resembles (minus the primary colors): You could turn this facade in any direction and still have an interesting rhythm. Basically flat, this residence's facade gives the illusion of depth based on a subtle layering of disparate materials and subdued colors, making for a clever and complex design in a neighborhood of 19th-century rowhouses and reclaimed storefronts that are now residences.

Architect Hans Egli built these minimal, boxy, faceted twin houses in 1987 on a difficult, odd-shaped lot that defied easy use for many years. The lot was first earmarked to be the site of a service station, then a 33-unit apartment building and, later, a convalescent home. Mildly echoing Moshe Safdie's Habitat '67, Egli's creations are stylistically houseboat, beach house, summer house and student housing combined – they were for their time and place (and still are) notably avant garde. Built from basic commercial materials, not beautiful per se, they are a battleground between permanence and impermanence, and what that existentially implies. There is a skewed symmetry to the buildings, and they possess some unusual touches – circular porthole windows, tile as molding around the entrances, an elaborate mirrored-tile mosaic on the driveway wall. There is something institutional, even motel-like, about them, especially the jutting balconies, the plain flush doors and the anonymity of the facades. And then there is a strange, central. meandering stairway that is like a dock leading down to the waterfront – except that there is no waterfront. These houses quietly revel in being out of context, and not only with their immediate surroundings; they also defiantly reject the architectural trends of their time, and the current one. They were hip at the time they were built, and are still hip and counting.

Here's another intriguing contextual juxtaposition from the drafting table of Hans Egli. This unusual house is a contemporary twin – definitely fraternal, not identical – nestled into a block of Italianate villas by the legendary architect Paul Cret (in fact, Cret's own house from 1913 is just a few doors away). Built on a corner in 1981, Egli's certainly has a fractured spatial sense. View it from one street, and it looks like a city townhouse with its flat facade. From the other street's vantage point, however, the side of the house unfolds into a surprisingly sculptural three-dimensional alpine ski lodge (Egli was, after all, born in Switzerland). From a certain angle the house looks as if it is half buried in its site and all that is visible is the roof and tower. The entrance facade is reminiscent of one of Egli's other works in this book (see *Modernist Assertion*): the large arch that is not the entryway, the horizontal band of windows above it, the asymmetry and playing with geometry, broad gestures with few details. There is an institutional quality about the tan split-block surface – a Modern Functionalism in which material is what it is and there is no attempt to hide it. And on top of all this, it is an eco-friendly dwelling with a greenhouse and hot-water solar collectors on the roof, one of the very few in the city then and even a quarter-century later. Scandinavian and forward-looking, even utopian in design, it displays a kind of international architecture of practicality, a solid social democratization that could be built anywhere, sometimes on green sites. Extremely individualistic, it has the look of "then" and at the same time, perhaps, the look of "soon."

At first glance, this house seems as if a 19th-century vintage townhouse was simplified or International-ized (smooth stuccoed facade, gridded windows with lively paint). Actually, though, it is a 20th-century rowhouse with an old-world reference in a circa 1850s Philadelphia neighborhood. The house was built around 1930 by architect James P. Metheny for himself, and was the start of the changing and gentrifying of a certain then-on-the-skids, now-trendy neighborhood. As a visionary in the 1920s, Metheny fore-saw and acted upon his strong instincts to revive the deteriorating city as a vital residential option by renovating and rebuilding city blocks. This unusual house, especially for its time, still seems modern in its approach 80-plus years later. In addi-tion, the paneled front door has somewhat quirky decorative touches having symbolism (the reason, long ago lost) of middle/northern Europe: some sort of Germanic heraldry images, either Prussian or Austro-Hungarian, very elaborate with mold-ing, specific iconography, and precise detail in the painting. This is topped by a decorative lintel with a molded design that may be linked to the door imagery. This unusual entrance creates an attractive and historic document of a very individualistic sensibility and its roots. It and, indeed, the entire house itself, act as a signpost erected by Metheny from the Depression-era past to help inform and inspire the future of Philadelphia's urban fabric.

Townhouses are all about squares and rectangles, but this 1960s-ish reworking of the concept is even more so; here, the top two floors jut out over the ground floor in a big cube, hovering above while also minimizing what was unusual for its time: a garage. The dark door openings create the impression that it's a box sitting on stilts or piers – a kind of dolmen-on-steroids effect. The materials used are rich and varied: pink brick and gray ceramic tile at the entry, custom fine-wood doors and detailing – a surprising use of wood in the city that is reminiscent of the work of George Nakashima or Wharton Esherick, which also places the house back in and of a time period. To the right of the double-row of International-style windows is a vertical line of glass blocks alternating with vents, acting like a dotted line or a directional sign pointing down to the front door – in fact, in a line plumb with the door knocker, peephole and centered doorknob. The striking vertical mail slot visually balances the stair railing. This is a cleverly designed building, emphasizing the cubishness of it all and yet balancing it with horizontals and verticals simply, carefully and artfully placed. Whereas most of the primarily 19th-century houses on the street are very much connected to the ground, this one gives the illusion that it isn't – as if the first story provides the primary function of elevating and emphasizing the above-street portion.

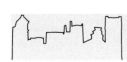

An environment that is too completely organized appears shallow in comparison, lacking spontaneity and a dynamic quality. If we find nothing out of place and if everything we see seems to have been foreshadowed, then our senses become dulled.
— **Eric Uhlfelder,** *Center City Philadelphia: The Elements of Style*

Be who you are and say what you feel, because those who mind don't matter and those who matter don't mind.
— **Dr. Seuss**

6

Quirky Individualism

In pursuit of their own particular and private Shangri-Las or Xanadus, a number of Philadelphians have built some undeniably unusual places in the city. The highly personalized products of eclectic — some might say eccentric — vision, these singular, unduplicatable, refreshing house-and-context fantasies go right past the viewer's analytical brain and straight to the muscles that operate the jaw: the jaw either drops in amazement or pulls up to form a broad, appreciative smile — and, in an anatomically anomalous way, occasionally does both at the same time. Many of these "beyond hip" expressions are thematic, almost narrative in their choices for invention and realization, but they are, each and every one, theatrical and uninhibited. Each property has a personality all its own. There is even, in some of them, a homemade quality. Each adds a jolt, a special-sauce piquancy to the city block it is built on. Yet, most walkers in the city will never see them, because they are on streets and alleys few travel down, which makes the imperative felt by the builder to build them even more wondrous to contemplate. These are no mere goofs or,

generally, the work of naifs — there is intelligently formulated exuberance at work here, and calculated risk-taking. Moreover, there is baring going on — of the architect's or owner's soul, of his or her heart, certainly of the right brain. While some come close to being design and improbability exercises, others approach the autobiographical. Denying the concept that most of the public has — that a house is just a place to do or put things in — these houses put something out. Most allude, in macro or micro ways, to dwellings or symbols or archetypes from other places around the U.S. and the world; these borrowed expressions, adaptations or add-ons are often far removed in tone, style or time frame from the buildings that they are attached to. Indeed, there is a wholesale ignoring, even denying, of surroundings. Unquestionably, there is the notion being presented that shelter can be anything one wants it to be. Simply, somebody wanted to say something in bricks and mortar, and he said it. The result has the air of oddity about it. And that's great.

There are any number of things one might expect to run into down a lonely and somewhat bleak, grafittied Philadelphia alley. A French chateau is probably not one of them. Yet there it is, with French doors, mansard roof, castle-like verticality: a quirky assertion of style and taste with no context for it, and little reason for most people to go down that alley to even accidentally encounter it. Hip and hidden, indeed. Built originally as the rear of a multifamily dwelling, then altered in 1961, it was refashioned, with a third story added, in 1997 by visionary Alan Charles Johnson's Alley Friends Architects. The feat performed successfully here is how this unreal place – classy in a strange, outlander way – somehow makes everything around it seem less real, and even out of place; if asked, "What is wrong with this picture?" you wouldn't necessarily pick this slightly Disney World-ish house but, rather, everything else in the picture. (It comes as no surprise that these diversely-talented architects have also designed sets for off-Broadway plays and horror movies.) It is, to be sure, an odd, sedate oasis that, in a way, couldn't be much more jarring if it had been a pyramid. Sometimes a house totally out of context can achieve near-greatness precisely because of its incongruity. This is one of those, a place that, when seen against a backdrop of the city's architectural big boys (including Academy House, which is one of Johnson's own designs), holds its own.

A conversion of two rowhomes into one urban castle (with a turret, yet), this Neuschwanstein-meets-North-Philly hybrid was a long-term personal project of architect Theodore Revlock, starting in 1986 and continuing into the 2000s. Or maybe it's an homage to the Midwest farmbelt, with its odd grain silo grafted onto the red-brick facade. Whatever it is, or means, or suggests, this home has a cultural importance, as it was an early herald of the rebirth of its neighborhood – a harbinger of growth and viability. Turning the corner into the little street it sits on, or seeing the glass-topped turret or the Wizard of Oz Tin Man chimney caps from a block away, you knew that a different soul lived here, and wanted to stake his personal claim, and felt that this was a good place to do it, and that it would be the same for others of like mind. Yet, despite the size of the project, and its one-off nature, it is a hidden, easy-to-miss treasure, and even more sui generis now than when it was first started, as all around it, and directly across the street from it, are new suburban-ish houses – the product of rampant "developeritis" – that fit in even less than it does. In fact, what Revlock did was not to modernize the place but in some way "ancient-ize" it – to apply elements that add history, but not necessarily the history of that building. It is like an archeological find bearing scars of time, and evidence of attachments long gone and additions that look like long ago.

Behold: Rowhouse as Hadrian's Villa, complete with hills and gardens. In a thorough rejection of the fairly non-descript 19th-century, English-influenced worker housing with raised entries and overground basements that it sits among, this house – which is in some stage of long-term work-in-progress-ness – takes its personality (and applied decorative scheme) from someone's idea of the glory of Rome. Looking a tad squat against the towering retaining wall it is built up against (and nearly seems to be a buttress for), this property stands tall when it comes to architectural accessorizing and iconic images: a coat of arms, lion heads, large coin-like medallions and a sizable Venus replica sculpture gazing down from a second-story niche. One might be justified in wondering if there is a lararium inside, or how many cubiculae it has. The whole place is a mason's dream: stucco, concrete, tile, brick and stone, all in keeping with its classical motif and references.

Next to the house, and carved from an oddly shaped, rock-encrusted hillock created by the strange relation of house and wall, is a landscaped terrace with a seating area, paths, a fountain, cast sculptural objects and a great probability of a grotto yet to come. In its relatively sedate way, this is an in-your-face building using symbols and icons of strength, courage and heritage to show the world that it is comfortable being what it is, no matter what you might think. It is an attitude to admire, at least in Philadelphia housing stock.

In 1949, in a previous life, this rowhouse was a multifamily tenement and tailor-shop storefront. The new brick front was started in 1979, and work continued for almost ten years. The style is a 20th-century take on Romanesque, built over an existing 19th-century structure, using the original striped brick to full advantage. Including as many arches as possible, it creates an interesting form. Long, narrow, two-story windows extend and connect the two upper floors' sashes, giving the impression that the building is taller than its three stories. The counterbalance of the horizontality of two cornices helps to keep it grounded. The first story has a more contemporary facade with a different color of brick, a cornice with corbels built to mimic the original upper ones and arched ironwork. A first impression is that it could have been a firehouse or is now a restaurant or florist's, or an undertaker, but is none of those. It is somebody's house, an amalgam of disparate and almost fantastical elements tucked into its surroundings of 19th-century vernacular rowhouses. Unusual, to be sure. Italianate? Or South Philly Italianate?

Architects Robert Venturi and Denise Scott Brown (who have no connection with this house, they would likely rush to inform us) have postulated, famously, on the idea of the decorated shed. Well, here it is, and more: a concrete bunker with a design explosion of diagonal marble tiles, cement lions, an ornate iron gate (replaced after 2006 by a steel garage door), all located under a gigantic billboard (erected 1976) that hovers over an expressway, making it seem as if the building had a crow's nest. A dwelling in 1934, the structure became a garage, then a print shop, and, now, since 1985, a residence again – redo by B & R Design Partnership.

Although it has, to our minds, no direct design precedent, it conveys a strange yet certain Mediterranean villa personality, with some classical references. The decoration is dynamic and vibrant, yet it also causes the building to recede, with the tiles (which cross through openings and nibble their edges) giving the illusion of shadows falling across the building's face. It's a place that defies categorization of taste by creating its own. The point here is that the residents could just have done nothing, but obviously felt an imperative to personalize, and it is not like anybody else's personalization. It is a singular place that takes joy in its own sensibilities.

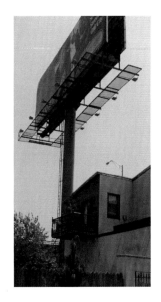

Creators of the faux French chateau (seen a few pages back), Alley Friends Architects – founded by Alan Johnson, Richard Stange and Bruce Millard – performed another geographical sleight-of-hand: they created an ingenious quasi-simulacrum of a Georgian Colonial house, something like (but not exactly like) what one might have found in an old New England whaling town, and seemingly airlifted it to a spot atop a multistory row-warehouse a stone's short lob from the interstate. Besides the playful incongruity (although it *is* near water, so some referential viability is at work here), there is the odd sense that the house is the old part and somehow, impossibly, the industrial building was built up from the ground later to meet it. In fact, the building has a long history, losing its top two floors in 1937, and transitioning over a span of 60 years from commercial to mixed use. The house went up circa 1999-2000. And, although it is near many well-traveled thoroughfares and popular entertainment spots, it is, because of its height, an almost unnoticed landmark.

Hovering in the air, the house has no ground around it, yet it has a picket fence; it isn't on the water, yet it has the makings of a dock, complete with looped mooring lines. One can even imagine a widow's walk, from which, looking out, one might see the past. Indeed, it's *all* a trick of imagination, with architectural history groundings – gambrel roof, dormer windows – revisited using modern structural techniques. This place simply should not be there. That's why, for the fabric of a great city, it is so necessary for it to be there.

There is so much going on here – so many different influences and possible references, so much about it that is of its time and of no specific time, so much about material and at the same time about ideas – and yet it all comes together into one coherent whole: the signature style of architect Adolf DeRoy Mark. Like some hippie-esque take on the Hanging Gardens of Babylon (sans gardens), this 1968 Mediterranean California Eclectic creation (one almost feels compelled to call it a contraption) was designed as a rear addition – with entrance on a small alley – to a much more conservative main building that fronts on a major street. The arched brick entry seems like something out of Mexico or Italy. There is a flowing solidity that starts at the top and follows a path down three flights of exterior stairs and into massive concrete footings holding up a deck.

In front of the footings there is a salvaged fragment from some lost historic building mounted on a brick base, taking the place of a courtyard fountain, and giving off an almost Mayan vibe. Clearly well planned, there is also something impromptu, something Haight-Ashbury free-form, even handmade, about it all. This is most evident in the amazing sculptural brick chimney (chimneys being a Mark hallmark), which looks as though it might have been moved to the site from the Watts Towers. Or that it is the world's largest patio chiminea. In all, this idiosyncratic place is a melange of houseboat and cliff-dwelling. In places it appears that its skin has peeled off and the inside is now outside, adding to its skeletal mien. It celebrates architecture by doing strange things with it, and for its location it is nearly revolutionary.

When western man left his cave ... and came to terms with a hostile environment his early home was no more than a structured cave with one opening; over the centuries this became a house with glazed barred windows. Then came the third stage with landscape as a friend rather than an enemy, and through the inventions of heating and large-paned glass, he broke down the barriers between interior and exterior.
— **Geoffrey and Susan Jellicoe,** *The Landscape of Man*

We cannot continue to believe that the landscape is sacred and the city profane. They must both be considered sacred.
— **Paul Murrain**

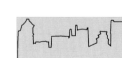

7

House = Site

There are few more intimate relationships than a house and its site – it would be impossible to imagine a higher and more sustained level of physical closeness and interdependence – and, yet, most of the houses one sees could probably be built on any generic piece of land, and most land would be fine having some other house on it than the one it has. It is a sublime and exciting situation when there is a full partnership between a house and its setting, a true equality, where one is so much a contributor to the other's success that it is nearly inconceivable that they not be together; think of Wright's Fallingwater as a supreme example. The hip and hidden places in this chapter, though certainly not of the monumental and iconic stature of Fallingwater, are the products of that same special, practically balanced interplay between house and context. Over centuries the relationship between human and nature has evolved. The most successful blending of the man-made and its environment shows a coming-to-terms and a chance for artistic dialogue that removes it from the ordinary. Unlike most country estates, where the landscape is a feature often worthy of discussion, all of these houses are in a city setting, though most don't look urban at all, and, in fact, appear to defy the idea of "city-ness." The connection of the house and the land, the mere choice of site and how it is treated with respect to the "intrusion" of architecture, how the site is used to compliment and complement the building, and vice versa – that is what this category is all about. It is about forethought, not happenstance; it definitely has the bigger, more complex picture in mind. It is about symbiosis, the mutually beneficial association of the one with the other, the close ecological relationship between a pair of living organisms – in this instance, the living, growing and changing organisms of a structure and its immediate environment. When done well and properly, the site adds to the complexity of the house; the house acts as a counterpart to its site. One does not overpower or subjugate the other. These are necessary, powerful and rare pairings.

This pretty, modest-sized contemporary residence, the Carner House, sits on a large-for-city corner lot enhanced by the beauty of its built environment. The house, in its simplicity, acts as a mirror to the garden and the loveliness that envelops it, becoming an element in the landscape rather than an object that just sits on it or dominates it. Sometimes it just disappears into it. At work here is a very Zen concept of balance, perspective and scale, including an illusion of space, not surprising considering the Asian touches of bamboo fence, pagoda entry (altered in 2009) and general attitude about natural vs. man-made. The house is an atypical cinderblock structure sitting among suburban brick and sided homes built for the most part in the 1950s and '60s as tract housing; its functional style sees materials for what they are, does not hide the structure with a decorative face, is very honest and forthright, yet quiet and unassuming. The architecture is suggestive, allowing for interpretation rather than forcing its style on the viewer. Danish Zen Modern, let's call it. Designed by architect Frank Weise in 1951-52 for the Carner family, who developed the gardens over the nearly sixty years during which they lovingly established their place. The landscape has all the essential elements: woodland with a stand of hemlocks, a perennial garden with an ever-changing series of floral displays including a masterpiece of a weeping cherry tree that embraces the entrance, a garden path that leads the eye but not the feet, a courtyard as sunken garden and a green meadow. The plantings are strategically placed to create distinct environments, in a very flowing and naturalistic way, leading the viewer on a visual journey.

In 2009 new owners restored the front portico to its original style (next page, top, second from right; far right is what it replaced), based on a photograph of the then newly built house and its occupants. The removal of a well-worn privacy fence and the addition of a referential wall (not original to the Weise design) that picks up the striping of the house's north flank are nice touches that even Weise would be happy with. Its Modernist soul probably wouldn't give a hoot about the site, but the two work so excellently in tandem that the effect would not have the power that is generated in this magical coupling of house and site. The varied garden elements and the house all fit comfortably within a fairly small footprint, an intelligent use of space that one won't find in most instances.

The site has been excavated, carved out to remove it from the street, creating a hollow and a barrier. The landscape is very inviting, and yet structured in a way to keep it separate through the use of topography and plant material. The bamboo panels form a folding screen; selectively placed, they do not encase the property and are decorative, not just functional. Even though this house sits close to a busy street, it looks like something one might come across while one is wandering through the Japanese countryside, and it is almost shrine-like. Unique house, magnificent garden, it's hard to imagine the one without the other – an exemplar of this entire category.

Like Heidi's house in the Black Forest, or something one would see on a postcard from a village in the Alps, or nestled like a Catskills cottage in a glen or vale with Rip van Winkle curled up inside, is this "country" house in a "natural" woodland setting. So deeply and perfectly set is this fairy-tale homestead that one would never know it is within view of suburban developments, radio transmitter towers and one of the busiest thoroughfares in the neighborhood. A miniature castle with turret and sharply peaked, triangular gabled roofs, it is all stone and wood, rough textures, patterned shingles, overhanging eaves and arched basement windows. The colors of the roof and the stone blend it into the surroundings, almost as if it had been created from on-site materials and built by elves.

A mixture of Arts & Crafts, Queen Anne and native materials, this 1930s house and the mini-piedmont it sits on show the interdependency of building and surroundings, and make clear that one without the other would not have nearly as much impact. The romantic context immediately surrounding the place lends it a storybook charm right out of the Brothers Grimm; one can imagine that smoke puffs happily from the chimney, even in summer, and that the walls are, perhaps, edible. A viewer can barely see the house during leafy seasons – like Brigadoon, it shows itself only periodically. Though a 20th-century structure, it looks to be from another century, another place: European, eccentric and unique in an overbuilt city. It's magical – a hip, hidden secret place.

Sometimes it is the contrasting elements, the yin-yang juxtaposition of the natural and the man-made, that make for the drama in and equality of a house and its setting. These two cubes, stark and spare, appear to be in conversation, whispering to each other in a conspiratorial way, standing in solidarity against the outside world where one building seems to be protecting the other, like siblings with absent parents. These structures have a body language, an attitude in which they themselves create a wall and a tension, angled like an open book that could slam shut, maintaining their own visual barrier. The landscaping is planned but irregular in design. There is a berm built up along the street with an assortment of wiggly, askew, "organic"-shaped trees and shrubs. The dialogue here is between an arrangement of two modern minimalist structures acting as a pair of hard-surfaced, blank canvasses, softened and brought to life by the expressive drawings and shadows created on them by the mounded planting beds and the erratic, St. Vitus-y shapes of the woody plants that surround, screen and animate them.

Since our initial discovery (pictured here), the exterior has been altered with a mustard-colored paint, giving it more of an adobe-style feel. Although the contrast has been a tad lessened, the effect remains the same. The first box (in photo above, on the left) was designed, in 1977-78, by architect Robert York and built by Distel, Inc., on land then-recently subdivided by owner Charles Woodward (see *The Pioneers*). The original site plan shows a more artistic/eccentric idea for the landscaping: serpentine rows of stacked hay bales interrupted by areas of crushed stone, a concept that was changed (for the better) by its now more effective use of contrasts. The second structure (above, right) was designed by the architectural firm of Bower, Lewis & Thrower in 1980. Connecting the two is a sloping wall, coming from the addition, which draws the eye to a point between the buildings, adding a diagonal tension. While the two structures are angled in relation to each other, the entire residence is angled on its site, so what we see from the street is actually the back, even though it is its entry. This house relates more to its site than to the street, and it uses its site to avoid revealing itself. It is an artful interplay between the built environment and the "natural" one, a perfect give-and-take between the two that completes the whole.

Like a house sitting in a planter, here is a home in a dense city area, with a setback and a front yard – a rare feature in an otherwise concrete-covered neighborhood. This residential gem, with its delicate balance of hardscape and landscape, is a modest townhouse on a narrow lot with a small (18' x 30') yard, and the two work in tandem as equals. The Mediterranean Style brick house was a renovation, in 1957, of an existing 1887 single-family home. Additions and alterations were made in 1995-98 by Brawer & Hauptman, Architects. Small though the front yard is, it provides a welcome separation from the street – a botanical barrier, of sorts. The yard and house are also raised up from the sidewalk, spotlighting the site as an elevated garden on a pedestal. It is not just a building – it is a little treat, a surprising green space in an otherwise right-up-to-the-sidewalk wall of brick houses. The facade is covered with ivy, extending the garden into and onto the house, making it look like nature is reclaiming it.

Because it sits back behind the street's other facades, the entry creates a courtyard feel, like being in a cloistered garden, or in a conservatory with walls. Such contained space extends the house, making the garden both an interior and exterior room with softened ivy-covered walls. Behind the decorative wrought-iron fence and gate, a flagstone path leads to both the front door and a brick arch to the rear, creating a meandering route into the house, something that most in-city homes sadly lack. The placement is intelligent, the blending of the architecture with its environment is balanced – one does not overwhelm the other but, rather, they coexist without making one less significant: garden and house have equal status – no mean feat in such a condensed, unpromising urban space.

Posed, rakishly, at an angle, giving you its best big, expansive smile, this house defies and even denies the fact that it is quite near a busy road and, so, it prefers to look elsewhere: toward the sun. Resembling a very large artist's studio, or a contemporary vacation home in Maine, the house projects out to the land, opens itself up to it and has plunked its modern self into this natural environment. Somehow it works by not negating its context, or ignoring it, but rather by just "being" with it and taking it in. The house takes full advantage of its site, and the site does the same — landscape and building seem in perfect harmony. Cleverly, the site focuses the viewer on the house, and the house draws attention to the site. It is a shared stage, an amphitheater built on the top of a rise in a woodland setting.

One smart result of sitting askew on the property is that both the structure and the lot appear far larger than they really are. The house, with its commanding presence and pared-down design, is not showy, and neither is the yard — no forced artificial plantings, no rolling English country-estate grass carpets are seen from the street; instead, just an elegant, calming blend of a coastal resort house and a cabin in the woods: Arts & Crafts meets International style. It was built, in 1952, by architect Harry Sternfeld, in whom the merging of a Beaux Arts traditional heart with a contemporary soul made this exceptional house and its superb relationship to its setting possible.

Art is the most intense mode of individualism that the world has known.
— Oscar Wilde

Architecture is inhabited sculpture.
— Constantin Brancusi

8

Artistic Assertion

What all the buildings in this chapter prove is that art transcends the merely decorative when it asserts itself and becomes a vital, inextricable element of the building — an element that, if removed or changed, would irreparably diminish the building. These examples are all purposeful expressions that either create from scratch a mysterious, theatrical quality that puts forth an artistic idea, or take an old building and "accessorize" or alter it in an artful and transformative way. In most cases it is not the architecture itself, the "bones," that makes you stop and look and wonder what's going on inside — it's the color or the object or the glittery array or the totality of the visual statement that does that. Think of the relation of sculpture, paint or mosaic to architecture found on Egyptian or Greek temples and, later, Gothic cathedrals. Those historic structures were the results of collaboration; it was difficult to know where the building ended and the art took over. Sometimes, on the one hand, powerful or polemical art can actually deny or overwhelm the architecture; on the other hand, at its best it can actually become it. In most of the instances that follow here, the buildings were a given, there was no collaboration between artist and architect, and

yet the result is an interesting and compelling balance achieved by the artist's assertion on a three-dimensional canvas. An expressive imperative can be achieved by many means: for example, through a sensitive approach to the use of paint, a surface application of mosaic tile, an organized system of "bricolage," the attachment of large sculptural objects or the original construction of a fully integrated conceptual design. Clever without being theoretical, fun yet elegant, artistic yet controlled and contained, often two-dimensional but sometimes creating three-dimensional projections, the applied designs enhance the complexity of their structures and go beyond the idea of "shelter," helping to explain and define it in a personalized way. Providing an attitude that is often playful and unabashed, an all-out effort at attention-getting but wholly deserving of the attention it gets, these dwellings did not need to be altered or built the way they are — that is why they are so wonderful. If the concept of hip and hidden is that of places that herald individualized expression, these artful buildings are among the most significant visually unique landmarks.

It looks like a restoration. It looks patched, and retrofitted. It's hard to tell which are the old parts and which are the new. Except … it's all new. This artful, triangular-seeming home is both referential fun (giving equal and eccentric acknowledgements to Classical, Colonial and Traditional Japanese) and serious design. Built to replace a three-story commercial structure demolished in 1962, this is an eclectic, modern work with a unique use of materials, spatial sense and overall sensibility. A quietly aggressive residence, it is situated in an architecturally diverse neigborhood of mostly 19th- and 20th-century rowhouses, as well as former shops and businesses that are now rehabbed residential properties. At street level, there is the arresting combination of gates that look like shoji screens (sadly, the driveway set has been replaced since this photo session) and postmodern lintels.

Look up, and a stepped wall guides your eye higher, to the wonderful white-stuccoed surprise "ruin" at the roof line – as if a wrecking ball had hit it, and then the owners had changed their minds and repaired the damage. This conscious effort of peeling back, exposing an under-layer, is reminiscent of mid-1970s Best Products showroom architecture, and takes a certain artistic license in creating a thematic, almost narrative exterior design. Theatrically illusionistic, from some angles the building seems to have only a front and no dimensions, like stage scenery, until you walk around and see that it angles off. Its profile resembles the prow of a ship, cutting through the history of architectural styles and leaving a unique vision in its wake.

When we think of "painted ladies," we tend to think of those frilly, small-boned and lithe Victorian Queen Anne houses we've seen in San Francisco and in historically reclaimed areas of other cities. This house is a different breed: brick, probably from the late 1920s (on the site of a long-gone 1794 structure), likely a former commercial building (there are indications of a one-time corner entrance, as well as nice apothecary-style windows), a bit squat, with the feel of a Mediterranean/Spanish jailhouse, or a posada. There is also a smidgen of the Art Deco about it. But what alters this building, what gives it its light-heartedness and its style is the exuberant yet judicious application of paint. The stepped roof line, arched windows, front balcony and display windows with overhanging roofs have all been enhanced by the teal, purple and rose trim and accents. Another designer might have denied its special character and chosen an "historic district" color scheme for it that would have made the property conform more closely to its neighbors, but instead the building has taken on a bit of New Orleans or Carnival.

Whether its "bones" are of a specific time and place, or the result of a series of building alterations and rehab decisions over the years, the way this house has been painted bestows on it a timeless quality, a look that can't be pinned down to any particular era. It is a surprisingly sweet transformation of a unique but architecturally undistinguished building (in a block of Colonial and Modern rowhouses) into something resembling a playful gypsy wagon – the bay windows acting as the side panels that open for peddling – missing only its wheels. You can almost hear the tinkling tinware dangling from its flanks. It is a fanciful place full of energy and style. Let San Francisco have its "painted ladies"; leave it to Philadelphia to have a "painted broad."

Imagine stumbling upon a sprawling, wondrous, found-object assemblage while exploring a tiny, cobblestoned alleyway. That is this place: part of a complex of old buildings and open space dating back to 1759, and which today includes a house, warehouse, courtyard and a monastic contemplative garden. Most of the buildings previously and, for three consecutive centuries, continuously had been occupied by a metal manufacturer/distributor. Alterations were made in 1986 by Roland C. Davies & Associates, carving out artist studios and apartments from the existing office structures. For the exterior of the other buildings in the group, reliefs and sculptural decorative pieces were placed all over the facades, making it feel ancient and reassembled, like the Elgin Marbles. A wanderer could be excused for thinking that he or she had come upon an ancient outdoor theater adorned with likenesses of performers of the day integrated into the walls. (In fact, the biggest of the buildings has been used to store the props and costumes of a local theater troupe.) But as you walk around the complex you realize that the huge number of objects goes beyond simple decoration and into the realm of artistic expression, or even obsession, as cast cement, stone and clay reliefs cover the buildings like barnacles. These objects are architectural artifacts collected – rescued, mostly – from demolished Philadelphia buildings, and all the objects were applied more than 40 years ago. Although amazing and even magical to view, it all makes you sad to realize how many terrific buildings have been lost, leaving behind only these small remnants.

There are moldings and wall caps, quite a few lions and images dealing with music and drama, perhaps historic figures, gods or muses. The effect is like entering an old mask shop that has amassed an antique collection – much as the Barnes Foundation has with its collection of metal hinges and handles, utensils and latches – and has decorated the display walls with a fascinating, eclectic and crowded array. If you had been told that a magnetic field emanating from the walls of this place had yanked these elements off other buildings and sucked them all to the source of the attraction, you'd believe it. That it was all done on purpose, presumably with some plan or at least some aesthetic principle, is what makes it all the more wondrous.

Art is about transformation: in some cases of a canvas, in others of a block of real estate. These two adjoining storefront properties, in a neighborhood of 19th-century worker housing that had been down on its luck in the 20th century, but riding high these days, is a mixed-media work. Like a complex – assembled, painted and decorated by an artist – they now house a gallery/residence that is an expression of renewal and revision. The facades are eclectic but cohesive, original and energetic, and are unabashedly about the idea of advertising wares – a big billboard for the tenant. A patchwork quilt of ironwork, stained glass, metal reliefs, painted doors and cornices, it is an overwhelming amount of design on reclaimed buildings that were given up for dead. Somebody took the time, energy and creativity to say something with it, to express hope and vitality to passersby … and, of course, to express her/himself. Often a work of this type is a self-portrait of the creator; here, it's one created sometime in the 1990s.

In 1940, to save the structure from demolition, the brick front was rebuilt. Nearly fifty years later, there was an attempt to use it as a boarding house for the mentally ill. In 1991, though, the place was taken on to use as an art and antiques business and two-family dwelling, and this is the result. Although this complex is not close to water, there is a feeling of the waterfront or the docks, a kind of seafaring reference to the steel of boat hulls, and how the rust of the windows trailing down the facade might be caused by salty air. It could be a sailors' pub. There is something in the imagery of the birds and fish reminiscent of the metamorphosis in an M. C. Escher print – an apt metaphor for what artists moving into, influencing and being influenced by unused buildings is all about. The upper floors are windowless, as are boarded-up structures, but the artist plays with the idea and takes it to another level, using the inspiration of an abandoned building and making it an asset, a beautiful point of the building. It forces us to reconsider what we tend to think of a house that has its windows covered, and how those windows are covered, taking a second look to see that it is not burned out or boarded up, but consciously artful. In the design, there is something that sums up what's happening with the dwelling and, by extension, with the entire neighborhood.

A bit of Barcelona's Guell Park on a flat surface, this artistic facade-lift to a three-story brick rowhouse, built circa 1810, is an expressionistic mosaic of tile and glass spilling out onto the pavement. It is reminiscent of the Watts Towers-style redos that one spies strolling along South Street, because it is the work of the same artist, Isaiah Zagar; however, this one seems more attuned and related to the current use of the building or the psyche of the occupant than just being festive or self-indulgent. Bold and blasphemous (in a hip and hidden way) in its context, this place is a welcome surprise in a modest neighborhood of Federal-style 19th-century brick rowhouses, some altered in recent years. The first story is the canvas for a fantasy collage of glass, ceramic and metal shards with references and interesting messages both visual and literary. For a print shop, which is what it is, it's a natural.

The building becomes its own signage that must be deciphered, that is not overtly stated and is an artistic takeoff on a "shingle" or awning. The backwards lettering reminds one of *Through the Looking Glass* – as if we've entered a mirror world; "the image mirrorical" on the wall is a Duchampian reference to his 1964 "Renvoi Mirrorique" engravings that illustrate the reflexiveness one experiences from looking at/interacting with a work of art. Other phrases embedded in the building's facade include:

"Walkers of the district that probe urban feelings"; "zinc plate and dreaming" (zinc plating is a printing technique); "sky clad walk" refers to wiccan/pagan ritual, with "skyclad" meaning nude or nudity; "unsolicited Isaiahs" and "close your eye" being typical acknowledgements by the artist to himself. Both attractive and meaningful, this rowhouse is unlike any other, and while the entire facade could have been covered with the mosaic application, it is far more effective in its limited and selective usage.

Once a purely commercial property – at various times a print shop, a ladder factory, a tannery and a trucking company – this building was, like the neighborhood around it, abandoned and in decline. Enter the artist. Now it is personalized, recycled, beautified and definitely unique in an area of 19th-century rowhouses and empty 20th-century industrial buildings. It may be missing windows, but it has what's important: the artistic imperative. Metal assemblages and whimsical sculptures hang off the building's second-story balconies like gargoyles. The landscaping, like the architectural ornamentation, is all heavy metal made light. This is not your father's welding shop; it's a jolly cross between a junk yard and a magic garden, with every decoration or addition made of industrial parts. Yet, with its metal bench by the front door, it looks like an old country store one might see in the rural South, the kind where nothing is thrown out and men naturally congregate. The zeitgeist is more about being a settler than being settled, and is not only quirky, playful, inventive and site-specific, but also a personal expression serving as advertising: a 3-D business card.

The work is large and masculine, not a mirror reflecting the viewer but a spotlight illuminating the artist; there is also something Vieux Carre about the designs, but here they are heavier and in steel rather than the decorative wrought iron one finds in New Orleans. The placement of the art on the large commercial structure affects the scale of both, each lending the other a kind of delicacy. The use of galvanized wash tubs as window boxes is a nice touch (ah, the feminine side), and this, again, plays with scale. A dismal spot made pleasurable and kinetic, it could be a theme park: Steel World.

This subversively circus-y place – people refer to it, with good reason, as "The Clock Tower House" – has so much going for it, especially pizzazz, that it is hard to know where to start. The amazing triangular brick and stucco building – fanciful in the way it's been restored and painted in a frenzy of color – sits on its site taking full advantage of its corner, creating a dynamic relationship with the street, much like the famous Flatiron Building in New York City. The primary colors of red, yellow and blue atop the white are Mondrian in 3-D, and the whole is like De Stijl meets Art Deco meets Pop Art meets Postmodern, at once overwhelming and perfect in its phantasmagoric expression of sheer joy. The colors most effectively accentuate the architectural elements – the stepbacks, cornices and pilasters – and are complemented by the addition of tile and glass block. New owners have, since these photos, altered the original colors, making some a bit louder, reconfirming our sense that it was perfect the way it was.

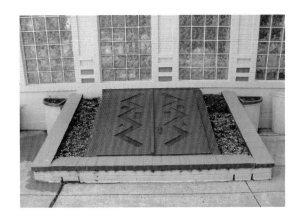

An original structure from the 1920s – at one point in its life it was a delicatessen; at another, a speakeasy – this 1985 renovation by architect David Beilman and builder Richard Dallett, which they designed to be "a caricature of the neighborhood," is now neighbor to mostly 20th-century rowhouses. (Another of Beilman's and Dallett's collaborations, the nearby "Ball House," is, they've said, a caricature of a different sort; see *Modernist Assertion*). Playful, beautiful, funny, loud, outrageous – it is all of these, but it finds a balance and even a kind of gentleness instead of going over the top. This house possesses a perfect combination of terrific original structure and what's been done with it (not to it) in application of a very design-y sensibility.

"

If for a moment we can accept Mies van der Rohe's slogan "less is more" as an influential credo of modernism, Robert Venturi's rejoinder that "less is a bore" can stand for the postmodern architects' counter-movement.

– **Thomas J. Misa,** *The Urban Machine*

When people oppose style [over] comfort, they are missing the point. Style is a particular kind of comfort. Something well designed offers a kind of psychic and perhaps physical comfort.

– **Terrence Riley,** *The New York Times Magazine,*
May 15, 2005

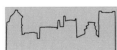

9

Modernist Assertion

The Modern period in architecture is generally placed sometime between the 1920s and the 1970s, a shorter timespan than that of Modern art, which began in the late 19th century and continues to this day. Both movements are typified by rejection of traditional forms. DOCOMOMO, the international group dedicated to the documentation and conservation of Modern buildings, defines Modernism as "an artistic and architectural movement that embodied the unique early twentieth-century notion that artistic works must look forward to the future without overt references to historical precedent," and which emphasized "functional, technical or spatial properties rather than reliance on decoration." It was a conscious movement, dedicated to purposeful design. The Modernist founders and purists saw their creations as utopian visions and set about to intellectualize and formalize the properties and principles of their idealized thinking to create, as William J. R. Curtis puts it, "a personal vocabulary, in which form, function, structure and meaning are bound together with a certain conviction and character of inevitability." Counter to its own hard and fast rules, Modernism — based on what we have seen — has become its own established style, or tradition, continuing to inform current construction, mostly public buildings but also residences. Those responsible

for the group of houses in this chapter decided not to play it safe in a traditonalist Philadelphia way but instead built new Modernist structures, many of which replaced something from a previous time period. All make forceful, uncompromising statements. All take Modernism seriously and, yet, aside from the theoretical, end up with compellingly handsome results. They are hip in their assertiveness as well as their fashion. Maybe part of their appeal is in their attitude of refusal to conform or to be predictable, or even to be "local," although many of these houses were built by architects of note who have been deemed part of the so-called "Philadelphia School." Some are already classics; others probably will be so in the not-so-distant future, but for now they are lessons to be learned from and enjoyed. Despite the Modernist dogma, there is undeniable emotional content in most of these dwellings. They are often insistent, always dramatic and more than a little aloof, with a love-it-or-leave-it, chip-on-their-shoulder arrogance that, when in an urban setting, tends to be utterly uncaring of their effect on the street and those who dwell on it. Like a confection, though, many have a hard exterior but a softer inner soul. They are unabashed design statements that are straightforward and relentless. Some are iconic. Some, surprisingly, are even cuddly.

In a section of town that prides itself – sells itself, really – on its many rescued, refurbished but accurately preserved rowhouses of colonial vintage, set on a cobblestoned stage of Founding Fathers look-and-feel, and feverishly protected by resale-value-attuned keepers of the culturally and architecturally acceptable flame, this Modernist intruder, built early in the neighborhood's renewal, must surely have been the Shock of the New. Retaining the facade material of brick, which not only prevails but is mandated for the area, this 1968 dwelling, which was designed for Mr. and Mrs. Howard Kellogg by architect Hans Egli (see *The Pioneers*), somehow accommodates, even reflects and emulates, its 18th- and 19th-century neighbors while at the same time ignoring and kind of thumbing its nose at them. It is a large-ish two properties wide, a biggish-feeling three stories high (although, as the photos show, it is exactly the same height as the house next door). It is, more or less, a giant cube, with artful cutouts and dimension, a grouping of interesting geometrical shapes.

The structure has impressive though not overly serious formality, and – though slightly fortress-like (or even modern synagogue-like) – imposing though not overwhelming mass. What saves it from being a red version of *Star Trek*'s Borg ship is the negative space, which makes such a monolith seem open and even airy: the small and large arches, which refer to the neighbors' arched entryways; the front door, which is recessed behind those arches; the huge wall of glass at the corner; the strip of irregularly shaped panes that ribbon along the underside of the inset; the row of eight windows at the top that, reflecting the sky, make that part of the building disappear. In addition, there are the "homey" and familiar, the softer touches, like the upright slate at the base that forms a planter for a small underscoring of green, and the trellis of wisteria across the large arch. Yet, somehow, perhaps because of its high walls, or its glass, or the horizontal string course of concrete that denotes the second-floor level within, or some sort of subtly shy dialogue with the street that is in many ways similar to its older neighbors, it is not unusual for a pedestrian to walk right by it and not even notice it. It has human scale, and that is an accomplishment, indeed, and quite a neat trick.

It's a simple place, but it looks like a lot of things: a school, a hacienda, something that architect Irving Gill might have built in Philadelphia – as if West Coast Desert Modern had met East Coast Preservation, an amalgam of old and new structures. Which it is not. In actuality the house was all newly built to look that way – a fine blending, an interesting illusion, an intriguing balance. This complex of connecting bungalows, low and sprawling with square windows, creates a modular design sensibility; meanwhile, the odd juxtaposition of the perpendicularly jutting stone wall gives it all an age-appropriate pedigree of sorts. Built in 1955-56 by architects Montgomery & Bishop and contractor Distel, Inc., it actually has the feel of an older vintage, as if it could have been there since the 1930s (which is about the time Bishop was studying at Taliesen with Frank Lloyd Wright, whose influence can

also be seen in this house), but it also has a timeless quality that makes it seem more current than it is. Despite it being a one-story building, the house has an imposing character because of the way it is sited. It asserts itself, even though it appears modest at first viewing, and because of its sectional nature it unfolds gradually to reveal itself. The stone portion divides the stucco portions of the house, and effectively hides half of it when viewed from most street vantage points; it also gives it an anchor, keeping it from floating on its roomy landscape. In another setting the more contemporary sections might even look like a motel, or the kind of socially-conscious group housing that architects Newcomb Montgomery and Robert Bishop were noted for, but because of the large site, the grounding stone wing and the split-rail fence, it resembles a ranch rather than a ranch house.

Truth be told, there can be a mausoleum-like quality to much of Modern architecture, resembling the simplified forms reminiscent of ancient Egypt. This house is no exception, with its near-windowless ground floor, its monolithic stone entry and its contemplative design. Quiet, beautifully understated, structurally rather than decoratively attractive, this Bauhaus-style residence with courtyard entry was built in 1962-63. In a previous life the property was a public garage, a bottling plant and a warehouse. At one time there were plans submitted to put up a 63-unit apartment complex in its stead but, thankfully, this design won out. Light, cool color palette, industrial materials, good balance of solids and openings, rectilinear planes and grids, nice give-and-take between horizontals and verticals (especially the lines across the limestone wall and the division across the windows) – this house has a lot going on in a small space and in subtle but assured ways. There is a layering of materials that creates simple complexity. Though there is something of the factory/office building about it (echoes of the land's commercial-use past), it has a kind of diminutive human scale that many Modernist buildings lack. In a context of Victorian, Greek Revival and Colonial Revival rowhouses, this hard-edged, yet not sharp, dwelling is a pure beauty, true to its ideas.

The yin/yang of Zen – the This/Yet Also That of it – can be one of the more stunning aspects of successful Modernist structures and their placement. It is difficult to think of any better, quieter, more dignified or more self-effacing example than architect Louis I. Kahn's Margaret Esherick House. Built between 1959 and 1961, the two-story, three-rank, stuccoed block house is a breathtaking combination of "hard hard" and "soft hard," concrete and wood, exterior and interior, light and dark, cold and warm, assertive and recessive – part man-made, part nature. Intensely silent and, in the way of Kahn, exuding an inexplicable holiness, the house – built for the niece of artist/furniture-maker Wharton Esherick – is a kind of spiritual fortress, sitting watchfully at the cul-de-sac end of a lightly traveled street, but separated from it by a sunken garden, from which one ceremonially enters the house; its back (similar to the front, but with more glass – see left, bottom, photograph) can be spied, with difficulty, only from the edge of a 10-acre public park which it flows into.

The Kahn signature concrete, the Esherick signature stained natural wood – some magic alchemy is at work here that blends these disparate elements perfectly, seamlessly. The place is rigidly formal, yet fun and alive – its central front entrance, tucked away in an alcove, plays peek-a-boo with the viewer; it thumbs its nose at symmetry (the two T-shaped windows are of different size and proportion) while seeming to be symmetrical – and seemingly referential to both Japanese and African influences. More than five decades old, it is still ahead of whatever curve it helped to establish. Like Kahn himself, the Esherick house is short of stature, tall in genius, rising above.

Like a geometric formation of white cliffs in the woods, this ultra-modern house sits on a hill and also on stilts; it resembles, in a way, a treehouse built out of concrete. Designed in 1990 by DDI Architects Inc., it has a steel-frame structure, wooden trusses and tilt-up cast wall panels. All glass and mass, the building is monumental, yet floats on piers, mitigating its blockiness and lending it a certain buoyancy or weightlessness. The glass-sheathed center breaks up the structure's solidity and divides the mirror-image wings. It is a bold statement quieted by its woodland setting – of which it has an acre to itself – as it peers through the foliage like an owl on surveillance. Totemic and silent, it also has a spaceship quality, as if it had landed in the woods and the t-shaped windows and angled porch are in mid-hatch-opening sequence, ready to reveal the wondrous other world within if one just waits patiently. Below the deck is a curved glass-block wall, to the rear of the house is a central pyramid skylight, and surrounding the driveway is a minimal amount of landscaping, raw and untrammeled nature having done the bulk of it. One of just a few houses that share space along this narrow lane that is not far from water, this unexpected structure brings to mind a cruise ship lifted into the jungle, as in Werner Herzog's *Fitzcarraldo*, or that desert-bound tanker in *Close Encounters of the Third Kind*.

This International-style dwelling, a massive Modernist house that looks like the stylistic progenitor of so many museums around the country these days (especially in the prominence of its upper windows, which appear to allow light to enter but not directly, giving a sense that the house was designed for an art collection), was built by the internationally influential "Philadelphia School" architectural firm Mitchell/Giurgola in 1963. The heavy, white, somewhat stark structure is tempered by the imposing weight of the site, a large wooded and landscaped lot of mature trees that obscures the facade's design but complements its hard edges; sitting on a rise, it is looming yet shy behind all the plantings. Known in certain circles as the Mrs. Thomas Raeburn White house — named for the client, the widow of a well-known Philadelphia lawyer, editor, constitutional scholar and government-corruption watchdog — it is all planes, every section like a wing, with angled rectangular solids jutting out from the facade: a fort built of multiple boxes. A sentinel-like structure, it seems the last outpost on a frontier of something — old-moneyed Philadelphia, perhaps?

What can we say about a place that has already been called, by more than one critic, the most significant house built in the second half of the 20th century? Well, for one thing, that it would be nice if you could see the darn thing. But there it lies, on a small and moderately-trafficked street that skirts a park (in fact, the same park that Kahn's Esherick House backs onto, just a block away), and down a longish driveway that ends in a wall of trees and bushes that, when in bloom, effectively block nearly every vantage point of the house. That such an internationally famous and uber-hip house could be so truly hidden is so very Philadelphia. Designed by Robert Venturi (then of Venturi & Short) for his mother, Vanna, and built between 1959 and 1964, this is both one of the opening salvos and the epitome of decorated-shed Referential Modernist (a better term, we think, than Postmodern) design. In terms of the American Dream House, this is the ideal and the abstract. At one-and-a-half stories, it is short, and it is compact – a cottage, really. But it is Everycottage, with its green-gray stuccoed exterior, its sharply pitched front gable and recessed center which is, in relation to the driveway, off-center. (The punched rectangular opening also looks like a car entry, making the place seem, at a glance, like the garage building to a main house.)

In fact, the house – which appears as if the contractors attached to the surface some of the architect's straightedge and protractor markings that were meant to stay on the schematic drawing – is truly asymmetrical. And playful, especially when it comes to the interrupted band of windows, linked by molding – normally interior decoration – affixed to the facade. It's a lesson in historicity, geometry (just count all the triangles, squares, semicircles and angles), de- and reconstruction and how something so simple can be so ingeniously complex, resonant and bright. It is an architect's dreaming mind made solid. It is certainly self-aware – perhaps even a tad self-conscious – but it is generally an odd mix of unassuming and revolutionary, modest and ambitious, plain and gussied up, urban and suburban, flat and sculptural, hot, cool and everywhere kinetic. We are participants in its totality because we take what is there to see and we add to it our memories of "houseness" and fill in whatever gaps there are. It pulls our recollections of "house" from us. It has all the language, all spoken at once, and sorted out through our filters. It is symbol and reality. Also, it's cute. If you could see it, you would know, instantly, even if unschooled, why it is famous, even iconic. Of all the hip and hidden properties in this book, it is just about the most of both.

Some people call this, for obvious reasons, the Ball House. Others refer to it as The Daily Planet building. But, according to architect David Beilman and his partner/builder on the project, Richard Dallett, this striking 1986 Postmodern redo of side-by-side rowhouse shells was modeled after a police precinct building, and is, in its totality, a "caricature of Philadelphia." Whatever, it is all mass and geometry, with the added theatrical dramatic flair of a humongous concrete sphere in possible momentary dangle on the cornice edge before rolling off the roof and crashing to the sidewalk three-sto-ries below, like a billiard ball in the corner pocket. This modern palazzo in a trendy rehab neighborhood is solid and solidly referential. Because the ball makes your eye flick upward (and, in a way, the ball does not weigh down the building but somehow lightens it, as if it were a balloon, or bubble, or a buoy), it was necessary to ground the place with horizontality – scribed lines, seams between blocks, bands of red and white – and with structural rhythm in the form of townhouse-shaped bays imposed into the centers of what would seem to be the walls of an apartment building, with a classic Philadelphia ambiance and coloration (with something Egyptian-like about some of the details). The entire project is a bold and eccentric choice, especially in the surrounding rowhouse/former-commercial-properties context; it is fun, but its bulk prevents it from being whimsical, or, certainly, trivial or campy. It is oversized in many ways, its elements (like the cornice and the corbel-like bay supports) exaggerated, and it is not exactly the most street-friendly place in the area. This whole building says, "I might be the product of today's architectural gesture, but I'm not going anywhere, and you better take me seriously."

Although hard to read – is this the front, the back, the side? – this modern structure has two really interesting things going for it. One is the horizontality and graphic window design of this shed-style dwelling; the other is that there is an artifact of a long-gone estate, a gatepost capped with an urn, that gives it a bit of contrapuntalism and acts as a reminder of what came before. Built in 1971 by contractors Distel, Inc., it's had several additions over the years: by Lorenzon Construction (1975); architect Oliver Keely and Distel (1977, 1980); and by architect Richard John Farley (2002). A modern stucco-and-glass series of grids, geometric shapes and positive-versus-negative spaces, it is hard-edged and without decoration. There is the oddity of the fireplace chimney and firebox, placed dead center at the entrance-side of the house, used as a dimensional design element within the very-windowed wall; the way it intersects with the L-shaped framing of the house structure creates a dynamic statement. This house has a stylistic simplicity that is reserved yet powerful among its mostly late 19th-/early 20th-century traditional neighbors and, like others in this chapter, its true life might be led on the nonstreet side of the house. Having been built on the site of a former, possibly grander domicile, there is its juxtaposition with the mature landscape, punctuated by the lone pillar, that adds to the richness of the mix. One without the other would not be as wonderful as the pairing is.

While Richard Neutra was one of the first and greatest of the European Modernist architects, his time spent working with Frank Lloyd Wright must have influenced him in terms of site sensitivity, for this house seems, in a non-Modernist way, to have been designed with this location and surroundings in mind, and its successful and seamless blending in with them. The Hassrick Residence, built in 1959, is so integrated into its setting – down a long, narrow, unmarked road within shouting distance but not view of a multilane highway, a park and a university campus – that it sometimes disappears into the camouflage of trees and undergrowth. This appears to be no "machine for living," but, rather, an entirely appropriate, cool-looking but warm-feeling home, one that, against all odds and its pedigree, says, "I come from here," not "I was put here." Indeed, its nearest neighbor – a nouveau French villa – is far more out of place than Neutra's is.

The house is one story, steel frame and masonry (with a band of wood above the garage, almost as a sarcastic jibe at its woodsy fate), shaped in plan like the letter "F," and it treats its inside and its 1.7-acre arboretum outside spaces as continuous and one. The addition of a George Nakashima-designed kitchen makes it all the more integrated in nature. Its street entrance is not its best face; that is reserved for the side away from the road, where one can gaze through large panes – protected by Neutra's signature overhanging roofs – into nature, or the direction of the designer swimming pool. Horizontal and compound-like, it has an honesty and lack of pretense, an informality in its presentation, a formalness in its design and elegance in its simplicity.

This might just be the most unusual and coldly impersonal residence in the city of Philadelphia. At the same time, this slightly scary, bunker-like dwelling, which looks as if the pavement swallowed it up, is like a box of Crackerjacks – a big square container, with a surprise inside, except this surprise comes wrapped in barbed wire. Mysterious, somewhat prison-like, behind its forbidding walls one can spy tantalizing glimpses of a cool, arty interior. The building is all mass, grids, horizontals, angles – a structure that is medieval and modern all at once – with a nice sensuous combo of materials: stone, metal, glass, tile, and a grisaille palette that is blue/gray. Built in 1993-94 by David Slovic Associates, it is a true Modernist building that has utterly no relationship to the rest of the street – or Philadelphia, for that matter: it is not pedestrian-friendly, has no landscaping, and there is nothing public about it, except in its role as its own massive and foreboding landmark.

The house's Material Functionalism is hard, cold, unforgiving, industrial, structural not decorative, and, yet, compelling and attractive in a graphic way. It seems visibly bolted together, an object to look at, a minimalist sculpture that resembles a helmet, not something to enter. The house has turned its back on the street, removing the occupants from the life of the city and giving them solely an interior life. This is not a welcoming place – looking, as it does, like the exterior of a Federal Reserve Bank – but is a welcome addition in terms of stylistic assertion and challenge, and its pure, cool attitude. Perhaps the most Modernist of our city's residences, and although philosophically wrongheaded in its connection to urban life, it is an artistically superior design. It lives on its own terms.

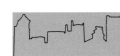

A freedom of choice for the future is best encouraged by a sensible, accurate and discriminating understanding of one's place in tradition.
— **William J. R. Curtis,** *Modern Architecture Since 1900*

No other city in America is so conservative or has kept intact so much of the work of each succeeding periods. It [Philadelphia] is a veritable paradise wherein architects may survey styles past and gone.
— **Coften Fitzgerald,** *Architectural Record,* July 1913

10

The Referenced Past

It's hard to walk anywhere in Philadelphia and not have the past all around you. Philadelphia is a city trying to not live in the past, but it certainly lives off it, and, because of all the vintage buildings that still grace the city, a lot of people live inside it. Indeed, because of the abundant stock of aged residential structures, and because of a respect for them, or reluctance to compete with them, or because of economics or personal taste, newly erected houses often tend to have their own look with no relationship to their context (the Moderns being the most extreme example of this). What this chapter spotlights are 20th- and 21st-century structures, newly created residential properties, that reference the past purposely as a design motif. Some quote or allude to traditional, representative styles within whose geographical context they exist; some refer to a specific historic style, while others showcase a composite of pasts; some pay tribute to a long ago time, while others acknowledge the more recent; some even refer to the past of another culture. Some play on a style with pointed references, some simplify and generalize, modernizing

and updating familiar forms, and others take off on a thematic journey that retains a connection albeit far removed from the original stylistic conventions. To casual and educated viewers alike, they all look or feel familiar, thus providing an intriguing comfort at the same time that they instigate an intellectual interest. Most are individualistic, intelligent designs that will not be copied, but they will all set a high bar for any new construction that follows on vacant city sites. These are not just new houses — these are new expressions of contemporary dwellings, and they all make some connection with historical precedent while attaining a clever, sometimes whimsical, often sublime personality that is all their own. Whether they are completely understood or not, they put forth a friendly and artful face where there could have been a blank one, or worse. They show the difference between the handiwork of developers and the thoughtful manifestations of architects (of which these all are), and by acknowledging the important role that historic awareness plays, they show us what we are made of.

Built in the early 1990s, this Postmodern Federal-style structure is actually an addition to an earlier house (far right, in the photo above, built in 1969-1971 by the firm of Hassinger & Schwam). This was no easy lot to reimagine: plans by architects Horn, Blyth & Partners (and Baker Rothschild) for use of the corner site changed many times between 1978 and 1991, from parking slots and a walled garden to a two-story addition of living space. The resulting clever solution is shown above, and on the facing page, bottom left. After 2005, a top to the garage and window reconfigurations were made by SRK Architects (opposite page, top left and bottom right). Each successive add-on has culminated in something more than simply happy or fortuitous: it is a little gem that stands alone as a real deconstruction and then reconstruction of classical elements, all resonating to the period of the original houses of historic Philadelphia that surround it.

It is a lesson in American architecture history, wittily illustrated, wonderfully fun-loving and serious simultaneously, playing with the forms and design details in new and inventive ways. The structure is a puzzle game, in a way, a Rubik's Cube in which the pieces haven't been put together in the "proper" order, but the way they have been put together is far more appealing, revealing and exciting. With a molded-wood beltcourse, denticulated cornice, louvered oval window, half an arch and stylized Palladian window, it winks conspiratorially at us, teasing us with its knowledge and challenging ours. It is not authentic but, instead, somehow uber-authentic, in the way good Postmodern work can be. Not only is it a reflection of a style but, when you look into its large quarter-round window, you can see actual original Federal-style buildings reflected in its glass. It fits in, and it is subversive, too. Intellectually alive but not a whit smug, it says to the viewer, "Tell me why I don't fit in here." There can be no negative answer.

A case of following one's own heart, no matter what the context, this 1987-88 project, designed by architect Edward T. Hinderliter, has a Postmodern/Miami/Atlantic City/Art Deco beach-house-ness about it. Set back from attached buildings – positioned like an old Jersey Shore rooming house, built on just enough land, squeezed between two other buildings – and with a gated entrance and short driveway, it has the air of a small motel, and it definitely has an attitude as though it had a view. The dynamic in the curves of the bays (creating almost a turret) gives the place a dimensionality unique among city townhouses, which normally relate squarely to the street. Moreover, this house, because of its convex facade, has a kind of axial rotation, like a lazy susan. There is a lot of positive and negative space created out of this small, rectangular chunk of real estate. The entry-level porch railing is glass block, and the way it overlaps and shortens the first floor windows is repeated in the design of the bays above; the first story is just like the second and third stories but rolled flat, the materials changing slightly but the design relationship remaining the same. With its sandy-color light brick, tubular-metal railings on narrow decks and its observation-decklike lookouts, it is reminiscent of postwar penthouse apartments atop New York City high-rises – something to maximize views at the top of the world.

Too many new houses in the city are looking like too many new houses in the suburbs. Whether it has to do with cutting costs, or an aesthetic disregard by the developers, a lot of new city residences appear to be blown-up versions of those plastic garden sheds sold in home centers: basically, a box with vinyl siding and faux shutters (for that quaint "Colonial" touch). There are exceptions. These contemporary twin houses could be accused of being too minimal and spare, given their context, but they are easily understood interpretations of classic city townhouse vernacular: "Everyhouses" with a sense of quiet style. These are an homage to the surrounding 19th- and 20th-century neighborhood homes reframed in a 21st-century design. Their basic form and size, the window heights, the stylized cornice, a suggestion of Victorian bays – all are rolled into a streamlining of the collective characteristics. Built in 2001-2002, these twins replaced a warehouse/rooming house that previously had been a stable. Designed by Richard M. Cole & Associates, the facades are made of stylish light brick (different from the neighboring red) with horizontal banding that breaks up otherwise plain faces and creates an interesting rhythm in the composition. A recessed entry continues vertically, giving depth to the facades; large paned windows become design elements rather than just functional holes, resulting in a rectangular arcade; and an asymmetry based on house widths adds attitude and informality to the facades' otherwise symmetrical demeanor. They are hip and welcome additions to the stock of Federal architecture, happily different from the prefab-looking developer houses. With a kind of hat-tipping to dentil mouldings of the past, they are like the old architecture with the wrinkles and lines removed; what remains is attractive and stylish, avoiding the potential pitfall of blandness.

This novel complex designed by Cecil Baker & Associates was built in the late 1980s by Miles & Generalis (of more recent loft-development fame). A stylized, contemporary, steeply pitched metal mansard roof descends from a clerestory of narrow windows and is practically right at street level, as if a portion of this building had been pressed down into the ground or buried (a la *Planet of the Apes*) to its uppermost story. We are presented with a finely structured cohesive jumble — a sampler of Philadelphia roof lines, brick facades and window styles, just minimalized or exaggerated in different ways. It is institutional looking, like a doctor's office, but more playful, like a daycare center; it assumes a defensive posture but also, contrastingly, a friendly demeanor because of the theatrical effect that gives passersby that Peter Pan feeling of flying above the housetops of London. Odd by itself, odder in its context, taking up a large portion of the block on a small street of 18th- and 19th-century townhouses, it is almost a newly-built New Urbanism town unto itself.

There is a cool hipness to the materials on these townhouses, an enterprising use of multi-textured industrial products, such as brick, cement block, diamond plate, corrugated fiberglass and wrought iron. There is also a reimagining of form within the very limited construct of a "rowhouse" – a playing with architectural language or vocabulary, including references to specific elements of the surrounding 19th-century buildings, making for a contextual jumping-off point. These three townhouses were built in 1999-2000, replacing demolished, circa 1840 structures. Designed by Cecil Baker & Associates, built by the firm of Foster-Willson, the houses went on to win an American Institute of Architects award. There is an illusional effect going on with the width of the houses as a group: they seem to be narrower than they are, or, perhaps, overlapping – the long vertical split that presumably separates the houses doesn't; the roof-line corbels indicate the borders of the houses, but nothing else does. This sleight of hand gives these boxy houses a more fluid rhythm and flow, breaking up the static block, linking the separate and minimizing predictability. The similarities to neighboring architecture include mansard roofs that are in keeping with those of the older houses but are, uniquely, made of fiberglass (again, as with Baker's work on the previous page, we are confronted with creative mansards); window heights that line up with those of the adjacent house; corbels and brick courses that are aligned with the neighbors', making them fit in even though they are contemporary buildings built of new materials. The cement-block framing around the garage doors minimizes the "garage door-ness" of them, while at the same time lightens the entire building, not only with its color but by, again, tricking the eye into thinking that the houses are built on piers. This is savvy design that has a sense of humor as well as style, referring to its context, yet still making its own statement.

This is not, as it might appear to be, an old farmhouse, now updated and modernized, extant before the rest of the neighborhood grew around it. Rather, it was newly constructed in 1999 by architect George von Scheven on a vacant lot that once held two twin houses. This odd apparition could be a historical reference to the sort of structure that might have been on the land here at the time of the earliest settlers. Oriented in a perpendicular fashion to the street, there is an almost suburban feel to it. Although the site is level, the structure resembles a two-story bank barn at the street side with two large openings: the upper resembling a hayloft (with the addition of a bracketed balcony); the lower, a garage door, where a great door traditionally would be. This plain and fancy dwelling – on a small, overlooked street of 19th- and 20th-century twins and single homes – displays a striking starkness of form. At the main side entrance there is a large, hefty pier. It is bloated and 'toon-ish, like Popeye's arm, or, rather, has the shape of an old milk bottle, and it supports a front corner of a shed roof. The other corner rests on a garden wall that changes direction and becomes vertical, making for an entry of sculptural asymmetry. Above it, an oversized dormer window looks like a second hayloft and the crowning cupola seems "original" to the "barn," with the parged walls, simple wood rails and gates all resonating the rural life in a pared-down modern design.

This structure – which is actually two cleverly disguised modern residences – relates to the street as a gateway. Built around 1963 by architect Beryl Price, with additions and changes by French & Crane Architects & Planners in 1990 and 2002, it has a grandness and, yet, a simplicity to its design. With a revisiting of classical themes in new materials, it is a collage of and homage to the past. It is much more horizontal than most city houses are, emphasized by a huge stone cornice and entablature, appearing to be supported by two pairs of stylized steel "lotus columns." There is an inset entry, and brickwork with recessed pointing that makes a textural, striated pattern. Call it Postmodern Egyptian meets Neocolonial, with fenestration and ironwork that makes it look like the offices of some farflung British delegation. At first glance the facade appears to be symmetrical, but a closer look reveals its asymmetrical nature, which helps to make it less static; there is an odd increase in the number of windows looking from left to right, as if the building were in an exaggerated perspective – one, a pair, then three windows, and all with increasingly sized ironwork balconies. The result is very hip, rigorously controlled and clever, respectful but free of the constraints of context. Although this dwelling has nothing to do with its neighbors, which are mostly 19th-century structures, it looks older, with echoes of long ago, but managing to be contemporary at the same time.

There are very few residences in the city that have a predominantly non-Western architectural style. This is one of them – and how. In terms of size, shape, attitude, origins or ethnicity, this 1982 work by architect Frank Weise is thoroughly sui generis. And it is completely unapologetic about it – true to its own wishes. Almost a desert mirage, it sits like the Sphinx, as a guardian, friendly yet protective, in an alert repose, surrounded as it is by colonializing but nonthreatening post-Civil War, 19th-century Victorian townhouses. Having the color of a sand dune and rising like a ziggurat from the pavement, this terraced, stuccoed, modern house with a North African flair even has its own mini-Egyptian-pyramid newel posts at its entrance.

The facade has Islamic details: the arched cutout at the second floor; the squarish shapes of the ground-floor openings with surrounding walls suggesting a courtyard at street level; the latticework on the door and deck, almost mihrab-like, having a symmetrical abstract pattern and screening effect (it also casts sunlit patterns). There is no dome but it could accommodate one. A kind of Modern Moorish Adobe style, looking like a stop on some trade route, it is a place to rest in the shade of a "tent," or its walled garden, and have some wine and figs. Monolithic, it is what it is. Marching to the beat of a different *dombak* player, this house is intriguing, exotic, mysterious but not ostentatious – unusual for a residence in Philadelphia … or for most of North America.

If cities were built by the sound of music, then some edifices would appear to be constructed by grave, solemn tones, and others to have danced forth to light fantastic airs.
– Nathaniel Hawthorne

A house is a human intention expressed in architectural and poetic terms. Through the architect man's collective memory of the past should be related to the individuality of the owner's life. Thus a true house, within a common language, becomes unique and is incapable of being reproduced.
– Romaldo Giurgola

Unique, No Comparables

In ten previous chapters, homes have been grouped under rather specific headings, taking the scores of houses that fit the overall "hip and hidden" criteria and placing them in aggregations of visual, thematic or theoretical similarity. Those in this chapter are the ones that didn't fit: the Magnificent Unclassifiables, the structures that are so different, so unrelated to any other that they required — no, demanded — a grouping all their own. Does being categorized the most different of the different, the most individual of the individualistic, make them, then, the best? Not at all. The hippest? Not necessarily, but they are definitely hip, and one-of-a-kind, and difficult to discuss, let alone comprehend. There is something fantastic, even otherworldly about them. No one would ever guess, seeing them out of context, that they were in Philadelphia — or America, for that matter. Some seem Old World European; some have recognizable points of reference. Oddly, though they fit in none of the other of this book's categories, many of them seem to be a little bit of just about every category, the way white is not the absence of color but the presence of all colors. All were built in the 20th century; all were architect-designed. All but two are built of brick,

making them, strangely, traditionally Philadelphian … at least in use of materials. They make all other buildings seem ordinary, even some that are most extraordinary. There is no explanation for them. They cannot be pigeonholed and, therefore — in addition to the fact that many of them are on the most hidden of streets — they fly under the radar. They communicate in some other language that is being spoken for the very first time. They are the embodiment of a vision, or, perhaps, a vision quest. They are unduplicatable, perfect islands that float in our midst but, for lack of understandability, are undetected glimpses of savant madness in a sea of conformity. These unusual houses are the stuff of dreams: the American dream of individual expression, the dream of creating a legacy that enriches a great city. As are most of the dwellings in this book, these are the unsung heroes, the pearls of wisdom that a metropolis generates because of the variety and eccentricity it embraces and nurtures. Such works have no comparatives, not even each other. Like inexplicable forces of nature, they awe and humble and help make life a string of tantalizing encounters. Without uniquely designed architecture like this, we would be a pretty boring place.

Like a big, sculpted, North African sand dune, this extremely modern Moorish entrance gate is way out of context in its post-Civil War Victorian vernacular neighborhood. How to categorize this 1980 invention of architect Frank Weise? "Postmodern Islamic Art Deco"? As if a gateway to another dimension, this mysterious, windowless, nearly blank facade has an amazingly simple and stylized design that speaks volumes. Broken up by line and color, it spans a wide stretch of real estate in a densely packed area and looks like a mirage of contours cut by the desert wind, or an uncovered entrance to a mastaba tomb. Since these photographs were taken, the entire wall has been whitewashed. Although it diminishes the dimensional effect of the two-tone version pictured here, its form is still very present. In fact, now the metaphor might be more akin to an ice palace, but its uniqueness stands.

A replacement for an existing wall – behind which was built, from 1970 to 1976, a house/complex created from several existing structures – its 15' height looks less foreboding because of its horizontal lines, as if the darker bottom were the gate and wall, and the lighter top the world beyond. This monumental entry is grand yet understated, with something mausoleum-like about the design and the quiet it evokes. The sleekly arched entrance doorway, as well as the three dynamic vertical grooves (one might expect a waterfall to flow over them), break up and balance the weight of the expanse, lightening the big plain wall. One's eye is led to the narrow, raised planting bed that suggests, perhaps, a glimpse of what lies beyond the gate. Utterly a one-off, beautiful and bizarre in a pristine way, not a house per se but part of one, and nearly big enough to be one; and, more than most houses, it has an unusual and powerful face onto the street.

This modern brick corner row-house has the unmistakable touches of "residence," such as a lion gate, a stunning front door and privacy glass; yet, it has the look and feel of something commercial, like a boutique bank or a contemporary addition to a library. Pinkish brick, stainless steel and glass block, together with a freestanding dormer, a porthole window on an exaggerated mansard setback above a recessed entry – all add up to an extremely nonconformist design that is both avant garde and classical in its references. Its overall design doesn't seem to have a frontal orientation; instead, there are lookouts or points of view from various places, but not one is dominant, making it seem protective and armored but still friendly. Considering that it is on a busy corner, it does its best to completely hide itself and contain itself, at the same time peering out from behind itself. It is unique among a mix of 19th- and 20th-century neighboring rowhomes. Built in 1979 by architects Baker, Rothschild, Horn & Blyth, there is something institutional about it, but, even more, something nautical: a strange hybrid of a boat, a store and a house.

Like a Cubist work by Picasso, features have been taken and moved around so that the viewer's spatial sense is altered, the design seems inappropriate and there is a theoretical playing with reality; it is as if the usual spaces of a "house" have been reversed – every place you think an opening should be, it isn't, as normally predominant features recede in this topsy-turvy but clever scheme. There are no typical guideposts, and this nontraditional house makes one lose all sense of logic and scale. Most of all, it forces one to think about the concept of "house" and what we assume that means.

Built in the 1920s, this handsome, reserved structure has the look of an old, small theater, or, perhaps, the headquarters of a medieval guild. Occupied as an architecture firm's office from 1927-37 by Edwin H. Silverman and Abraham Levy, the abbey-like building is now residential. It has an undulating tile roof, brick arches, a classic Corinthian column with a double arch at the entry and, directly above the column, a circular ceramic tile with the image of an artisan at a drafting table under the word "Architecture." The old world echoes are undeniable.

The Lombard Romanesque style of the building (which resembles some of the firehouses erected in the city around its same time) is distinctive for a house. There is a real sense here of time standing still, as if this place had been and continues to be a cathedral of learning, a center of scholasticism, where one might be greeted by friars, or might find applied-arts craftsmen seated at elevated desks. This house stands removed from, although attached to, its 19th-century vernacular neighbors, nestled quietly in their midst with an unassuming scale, but a grand and welcoming openness and sense of style – an intriguing, lasting and charming reminder of a building that once was inhabited by architects and branded for all time as architecture.

In this indefinably unusual house, its front and its back are so astonishingly different, they could be two separate houses built tight against each other – to the design chagrin of each. The only thing the back and front have in common is construction material: they are faced with white stucco, something that isn't typical in wide areas of Philadelphia, or even in this place's immediate surroundings. The stucco on the front is strangely, eccentrically bumpy or blobby, punctured occasionally with small protruding windows, but mostly flowing, bubblingly, down to a terrazzo sidewalk and a below-ground entry. Call it Modern Alamo Adobe style, or say that it looks like it was carved from snow.

Stark, soft yet hard, the house — built by architect Morris Schwartz in 1966-67 — resembles chenille or an impasto painting, a wax model or a homemade cake with thick icing (that, as in MacArthur Park, someone left out in the rain). The other, rear facade is a smooth sand finish and in the International style, like something one might have come upon in a rich and daring Parisian arrondisement in the 1930s. The crowning touch to this side of the house, if you look up from the next street at just the right angle, is a terrifically surprising Victorian rooftop conservatory. The deck off the second story was added, in 1982, by David Wisdom & Associates. It appears almost as if the rear is the way the house was meant to be, and the front has either been eroded or thawed by the elements; of course, it is intentional, like a contemporary wattle and daub technique, a kind of parched earth, but without the cracks. One need not fear contradiction in calling this house one-of-a-kind, atypical even on what is an atypical block, for Philadelphia, of recent-vintage construction and Spanish Mission-style re-dos from the late 1960s. A mixed metaphor with notes of Modernism, but also with an overlay of primitivism, it is concurrently futuristic and prehistoric — cavelike, really, with its excavated entrance, the texture as if it were natural rock that's been whitewashed or coated, and then chiseled into.

Situated in a historically significant part of Philadelphia, this house has its own sense of historical reference – one that harkens back more to medieval than Georgian England. This is a mini-castle in the city. The first thing one notices, besides the style, is that the building is rounded – a luxury for a city structure, because of limited space – and also recessed. It is sculptural in a mostly flat environment. This turreted townhouse was built – on a lot that lay vacant for a dozen years – by architect Adolf DeRoy Mark in 1972, in a setting of circa 1830s rowhouses, most of which were being redone around the same time and later. But not quite in the same fashion. Looking as if there might be a drawbridge concealed in there somewhere, the entrance is enclosed by a decorative iron gate that looks forged and that defines and separates access from the street, making it feel processional.

Besides the Flemish Bond brick design, the sash has bubble glass at ground level; a small, curved balcony covers the entry; large-scale gaslights grace each porch; arches carry the eye up into a more Spanish-style, stuccoed portion with a Mark-signature narrow, towering chimney; and a carved or cast ram's-head relief graces the tower as a gargoyle might. There is something Shakespearean about the facade, and not just because of its Juliet balcony. This house, though out of place among its more conservative neighbors, blends in … a bit, while evoking a fairytale world of chivalry, strength and protective armor in a design that shows the street that all the world's a stage.

The houses next to it, across from it, all up and down the street are Colonial- or Tudor-revival styles. This one isn't – not by a long shot. This modern day mastaba looks like the new branch library for the community. With a horizontal orientation and a recessed ground floor, it hovers like a spaceship, an alien in the midst. Built in 1968, it was designed by Norman N. Rice, an architect who was a colleague and friend of, and co-teacher in a master's studio at the University of Pennsylvania with, Louis Kahn, and worked in the offices of Paul Cret, Le Corbusier, Jose Luis Sert and Howe & Lescaze (while they were working on the PSFS Building). He also had an interesting take on things: this place is just absolutely different from anything in view, somewhat robotic-looking, is its own thing and makes no attempt to blend in.

Its front looks like a back; the entry, although delineated by brick piers, could be mistaken for a rear door or service entrance — twin doors separated by a vertical line of single glass blocks. Until recently, with ownership change, each glass block contained, for obscure and fascinating reasons, a toy bunny — a fanciful and welcome bit of lightheartedness in an otherwise serious design. The structure gives the impression of sitting on stilts, and it creates an architectural tension and balance within its rather plain masonry box through the interplay between horizontal mass and vertical elements (such as the long narrow windows) — an East Coast homage, perhaps, to Le Corbusier's Villa Savoye. This house not only has character but *is* a character, peering out from its lush, green, camouflaged fortification with a big toothy grin.

This stronghold-like house exudes a Middle Ages feeling similar to what one experiences when viewing the Moravian Pottery & Tile Works, but with a 1960s Spanish/California spin (and several colors of weathered-looking brick rather than concrete). The house has an excavated basement entrance and a remarkably tall and tapered chimney with a keyhole opening at its hood. There are four large arches across the front – recalling a medieval walled town, with its limited-access gateways – each with a different function: one leads to stairs going up, another to stairs going down, a third is an alleyway that sidles along the flank and the very large fourth has ironwork that resembles chain mail, and behind which is a curtained window that offers tantalizing glimpses of what lies within. The entire structure unfolds as if it were an exploded view of a house – there is a layering, and the levels present themselves in a perspectival progression through space and time: as the building steps back and adds height with additional stories it also moves from the most ancient-looking part at ground level to the most modern-looking at the top.

This house makes the viewer work a little to "get it." The reason has to do with the way it plays with space and spatial issues in a far different way from most other houses in its area and, frankly, in the city. It is interesting to conjecture that, as one of the early new houses in its then-just-gentrifying, still slightly "iffy" neighborhood, it was built this way for a purpose beyond the aesthetic – for security reasons, perhaps. It seems to obscure and lead at the same time – to beckon and yet hold at arms length. It takes pleasure in making the simple act of entering a house a decision and a game. It also likes to be suggestive of other things: for example, the design, with the large central arch and the odd, exaggerated chimney – not to mention the "screen" – makes the whole thing look like a giant fireplace or kiln, enforcing the relationship of hearth and home. Another idiosyncratic castle-in-the-city by architect Adolf DeRoy Mark, built in 1973 amidst 18th- to 20th-century rowhouses, it is both contemporary and archaic.

We call this the "Architect's House" for two key reasons. First, it was built between the mid-1960s to about 1970, with continued work into the late 1990s – on the spot where a carriage house once stood – by architect Frank Weise as his own home. Another reason: Reflecting years of design process and evolution, it looks like a laboratory for architectural practice, a theoretical and experimental legacy to the city. Resembling nothing less than a beehive, there probably have never been as many arches in any one building, except, perhaps, for the Colosseum; the effect is like that of an enormous honeycomb. With this place, Weise might have been working out ideas on load-bearing, with the result that this multilevel layer-cake of a facade has all kinds of unusual shapes coming together to complete the whole. At the bottom is a spare, modern, recessed brick entrance, resembling a loading-dock, with massive piers and a kind of cold and unfriendly portal rescued by a smattering of wood. The second-story section might possibly be a reimagining of a Roman aqueduct; or, perhaps, the four layers of eleven arches each are staggered and tightly packed so that they can act, in a sense, as mullions separating panes on a giant window, reflecting yet fracturing the distant treetops.

At the top of the house is a trapezoidal structure with polygonal-shaped windows atop more arches – a hyperthyroid mansard sitting above an oversized protruding cornice. And there is a thoroughly unanticipated hoist and pulley, which harkens symbolically back to the original carriage house. The place seems to be commenting on and exaggerating certain classic architectural forms. Although the different layers don't seem connected, everything works together in this coy yet gutsy assemblage of balances and counterbalances, not only of weight but of style. This house

grabs its site and is not a novelty but a relentlessly challenging work of art. Had Weise wanted it to be confrontational, or even famous, he would have built it on a major street, not tucked it down a tiny alley – situated between commercial-style residential properties in a context of backyards and carriage houses. Then again, its great impact partially relies on the fact that one spies it for the first time as a kind of accident, a sidelong glance that makes one stop and make the effort to investigate this unique, personal creation – a thought-provoking and mind-blowing vision.

Neighborhood Guide

This is a general guide to the neighborhoods in which the hip and hidden houses in this book can be found, for the most part based on the neighborhood parameters set out by Kenneth Finkel in his 1994 *Philadelphia Almanac and Citizens' Manual,* as can be seen at the website *http://www.phila.gov/phils/Docs/otherinfo/placname.htm.*

While this is not a specific street-and-address guide to the houses, we hope that it will entice the reader to explore these areas and, while in search of the hip and hidden properties we have displayed here, to find new places, different houses and a greater enjoyment and appreciatiion of the city of Philadelphia.

Bella Vista (between 6th and 11th streets, South Street to Washington Avenue)
Pages 29; 30; 67

Center City East (8th Street to Broad Street, Spring Garden Street to South Street)
Pages 40; 48-49; 82; 136-137; 144; 145

Center City West (Broad Street to the Schuylkill, Spring Garden Street to South Street)
Pages 12-13; 14-15; 16-17; 28; 32-33; 41; 52-53; 56; 57; 58-59; 62; 64; 65; 72-73; 78; 79; 125; 147; 156-157; 158-159; 166-167

Chestnut Hill (Northwestern Avenue to Cresheim Creek, Forbidden Drive to Stenton Avenue)
Pages 18-19; 22-23; 70-71; 98-99; 124;126-127; 129; 130-131; 133; 146

East Falls (east side of the Schuylkill to Wissahickon Avenue, Lincoln Drive to Route 1)
Pages 134-135; 162-163

Fairmount (west of Broad Street, between Girard Avenue and Spring Garden Street)
Pages 44; 60; 148-149; 152-153

Fishtown (along the Delaware River below Kensington, Frankford Avenue on the west and Norris Street at the northeast)
Pages 112-113

Mount Airy (between Johnson Street and Cresheim Creek, Wissahickon Creek and Stenton Avenue)
Pages 20-21; 74; 102-103; 128

Northern Liberties (north of Spring Garden Street to approximately Girard Avenue, the Delaware River to Sixth Street)
Pages 35; 42-43; 83; 87; 116-117

Old City (bounded by the Delaware River and 4th Street, Spring Garden Street to Walnut Street)
Pages 88-89; 110-111; 114-115

Queen Village (from the Delaware River to the east side of 6th Street, and from and including the south side of Lombard Street to the north side of Washington Avenue)
Pages 26-27; 34; 36-37; 45; 66; 75; 86; 100-101; 106-107; 108-109; 118-119; 132; 142; 143

Roxborough/Manayunk/Wissahickon (between the Schuylkill, Wissahickon Creek and northwest city border)
Pages 31; 46-47; 84-85; 94-95; 96-97

Society Hill (Walnut Street to Lombard Street, Delaware River to 8th Street)
Pages 50-51; 61; 63; 90-91; 122-123; 140-141; 154-155; 160-161; 164-165

Spruce Hill (west of the University of Pennsylvania, Locust Street to Woodlands Cemetery, to the vicinity of 46th Street)
Pages 76; 77

Architects & Builders List

Alley Friends Architects
(see also Johnson, Alan Charles;
Stange, Richard; Millard, Bruce)
    Adaptive Reuse, 33
    Quirky, 82; 88-89

Amburn/Jarosinski
    Adaptive Reuse, 30
    Facelift, 61

B & R Design Partnership
    Quirky, 87

Baker, Cecil & Associates
(see also Baker, Rothschild, Horn & Blyth)
    Referenced Past, 144; 145

Baker, Rothschild, Horn & Blyth
(see also Blyth, Alden)
    Pioneers, 75
    Referenced Past, 140-141
    Unique, No Comparables,
    154-155

Beardsley, Christopher
    Facelift, 65; 67

Beilman, David
    Artistic Assertion, 118-119
    Modernist Assertion, 132

Bishop, Robert
(see also Montgomery & Bishop)
    Modernist Assertion, 124

Blyth, Alden
(see also Baker, Rothschild, Horn & Blyth)
    Pioneers, 75

Bower, Lewis & Thrower
    House=Site, 98-99

Boyd, Lawrence V.
    Adaptive Reuse, 31

Brawer & Hauptman, Architects
    Pioneers, 72-73
    House=Site, 100-101

Brosz, Paul A.
    Classics, 18-19

Cridland, Charles
    Classics, 18-19

Cole, Richard M. & Associates
    Referenced Past, 143

Dallett, Richard
    Artistic Assertion, 118-119
    Modernist Assertion, 132

Davies, Roland C. & Associates
    Artistic Assertion, 110-111

Day, Kenneth M.
    Pioneers, 70-71

DDI Architects Inc.
    Modernist Assertion, 128

Di Benedetto, John
    Pioneers, 70-71

Distel, Inc.
    House=Site, 98-99
    Modernist Assertion, 133

Egli, Hans
    Pioneers, 76; 77
    Modernist Assertion, 122-123

Eyre, Wilson, Jr.
    Classics, 18-19

Farley, Richard John
    Modernist Assertion, 133

Fey, Ralph C.
    Incorporated Past, 45

Architects & Builders List (cont'd)

Foster-Wilson
  Referenced Past, 145

French & Crane Architects & Planners
  Referenced Past, 147

Furness, Frank
(see *also* Furness & Hewitt)
  Classics, 12-13

Furness & Hewitt
  Classics, 12-13

Giurgola, Romaldo
(see *also* Mitchell/Giurgola)
  Adaptive Reuse, 33

Goldner, Stephen Mark (SMGA)
  Adaptive Reuse, 26-27

Hall, A.J.
  Classics, 16-17

Hassinger & Schwam
  Referenced Past, 140-141

Hinderliter, Edward T.
  Referenced Past, 142

Holm, Alvin
  Incorporated Past, 44

Horn, Blyth & Partners
(see *also* Baker, Rothschild, Horn & Blyth; Blyth, Alden)
  Referenced Past, 140-141

Howe, George
(see *also* Mellor, Meigs & Howe)
  Classics, 14-15; 22-23

Hoxie & Button
  Adaptive Reuse, 36-37

Jacobson, A. & Sons
  Pioneers, 72-73

Johnson, Alan Charles
(see *also* Alley Friends Architects)
  Quirky, 82; 88-89

Kahn, Louis I.
  Modernist Assertion, 126-127

Keely, Oliver
  Modernist Assertion, 133

Kruhly, James Oleg
  Facelift, 64

Krumholz, Kurt
(see *also* SRK Architects)
  Referenced Past, 140-141

Levy, Abraham
(see *also* Silverman, Edwin H.)
  Unique, No Comparables, 156-157

Lloyd, John & Associates
  Incorporated Past, 50-51

Lorenzon Construction
  Modernist Assertion, 133

Mark, Adolf DeRoy
  Adaptive Reuse, 34
  Quirky, 90-91
  Unique, No Comparables, 160-161; 164-165

McAleer, James
(*of* McAleer & Burkmire)
  Incorporated Past, 46-47

McDonald, Tim
  Incorporated Past, 42-43

McHugh, Thomas
  Facelift, 58-59

Architects & Builders List (cont'd)

Medoff, D.
Facelift, 57

Mellor, Meigs & Howe
Classics, 22-23

Metheny, James
Classics, 16-17
Pioneers, 78

Miles & Generalis
Referenced Past, 144

Millard, Bruce
(see also Alley Friends Architects)
Quirky, 88-89

Mitchell/Giurgola
(see also Giurgola, Romaldo)
Adaptive Reuse, 32-33
Modernist Assertion, 129

Montgomery & Bishop
(see also Montgomery, Newcomb;
Bishop, Robert)
Modernist Assertion, 124

Montgomery, Newcomb
(see also Montgomery & Bishop)
Modernist Assertion, 124

Nelson & Associates
Facelift, 66

Neutra, Richard
Modernist Assertion, 134-135

Nolen, James A., Jr.
The Classics, 20-21

Owens, John
Classics, 18-19

Price, Beryl
Referenced Past, 147

Regnier, Julie
Incorporated Past, 46-47

Revlock, Theodore
Quirky, 83

Rice, Norman N.
Unique, No Comparables,
162-163

Rosenthal, Morris J.
Adaptive Reuse, 28

Sauer, Louis
Facelift, 63

Schwartz, Morris
Unique, No Comparables,
158-159

Silverman, Edwin H.
(see also Levy, Abraham)
Unique, No Comparables,
156-157

Slovic, David, Associates
Modernist Assertion, 136-137

Sperr, Otto
(as Otto Sperr Associates)
Adaptive Reuse, 33

SRK Architects
(see also Krumholz, Kurt)
Referenced Past, 140-141

Stange, Richard
(see also Alley Friends Architects)
Quirky, 88-89

Sternfeld, Harry
Facelift, 58-59
House=Site, 102-103

Street, J. Fletcher
Incorporated Past, 48-49

Architects & Builders List (cont'd)

Todd, Thomas A.
Pioneers, 74

Venturi & Short
Modernist Assertion, 130-131

Venturi, Robert
(see *also* Venturi & Short)
Modernist Assertion, 130-131

von Scheven, George
Referenced Past, 146

Weise, Frank
Incorporated Past, 41
House=Site, 94-95
Referenced Past, 148-149
Unique, No Comparables,
152-153; 166-167

Wigham, Edward H.
Incorporated Past, 52-53

Williams, David
Facelift, 65

Wisdom, David & Associates
Unique, No Comparables,
158-159

Woodring, Greg
Classics, 18-19

York, Robert
House=Site, 98-99

Selected Bibliography

Burden, Ernest. *Illustrated Dictionary of Architectural Preservation.* New York: McGraw-Hill, 2004.

Burke, Bobbye, Otto Sperr, Hugh J. McCauley and Trina Vaux. *Historic Rittenhouse: A Philadelphia Neighborhood.* Philadelphia: University of Pennsylvania Press, 1985.

Cerwinske, Laura. *Tropical Deco: The Architecture and Design of Old Miami Beach.* New York: Rizzoli, 1981.

Curtis, William J. R. *Modern Architecture Since 1900.* Upper Saddle River, NJ: Prentice Hall, 1996.

DOCOMOMO US – International Working Party for the Documentation and Conservation of Buildings, Sites and Neighborhoods of the Modern Movement, *http://www.docomomo-us.org/*

McLendon, Sandy. "A 1936 Art Deco House Gets Back Its Luster," *Old-House Interiors*, March/April 2007, pp. 66-72.

Misa, Thomas J. "Modern Architecture and Building Technology: Literature Review." Illinois Institute of Technology, *http://www.tc.umn.edu/~tmisa/toe20/urban-machine/complete-pwd.pdf*

Philadelphia Architects and Buildings, *http://www.philadelphiabuildings.org/pab/*

Philadelphia Department of Licenses and Inspections, Zoning Archive, *http://www.phila.gov/zoningarchive/*

Popkin, Nathaniel R. *Song of the City: An Intimate Portrait of the American Urban Landscape.* New York: Four Walls Eight Windows, 2002.

Poppeliers, John C. and S. Allen Chambers Jr. *What Style is It?* Hoboken: John Wiley & Sons, 2003.

Schwartz, Helen. *The New Jersey House.* New Brunswick, NJ: Rutgers University Press, 1990.

Teitelman, Edward and Richard W. Longstreth. *Architecture in Philadelphia: A Guide.* Cambridge and London: The MIT Press, 1981.

"The Way We Live Now," special issue of *The New York Times Sunday Magazine*, May 15, 2005.

Thurman, Judith. "This Old House," *The New Yorker*, December 1, 2003, pp. 112-115.

Uhlfelder, Eric. *Center City Philadelphia: The Elements of Style.* Philadelphia: University of Pennsylvania Press, 1984.

University of Pennsylvania, Architectural Archives, Exhibitions, "Only Controversial and Not Detrimental: The Legacy of Modern Design in Chestnut Hill, Philadelphia," Kroiz Gallery, October 31, 2003–May 2004. *http://www.design.upenn.edu/archives/archives/chestnuthill.htm*

Webster, Richard. *Philadelphia Preserved.* Philadelphia: Temple University Press, 1981.

visit us at:
www.probascohauspress.com